EXCUSE ME. I'D LIKE A SHORTCAKE AND A CHOCOLATE CAKE.
YES, SIR!
is run by a bear.
HOW ABOUT TWENTY YEN?
BAMF
THAT'S TOO LOW!
THEN... HOW ABOUT THWIRTY YEN?
I THINK YOU SHOULD SELL THEM FOR **THREE HUNDRED** EACH.
CAN I WEALLY HAVE THIS MANY SILVER MONIES?
WOAH..
I THINK I'LL SHOW HIM A FIVE-HUNDRED-YEN COIN NEXT TIME.

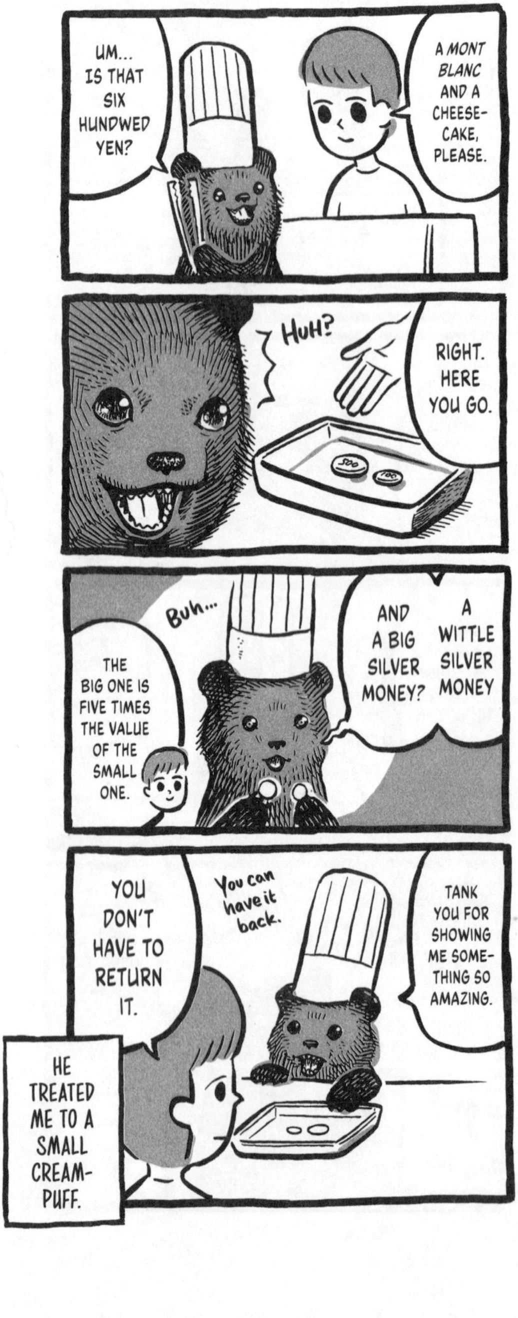
A MONT BLANC AND A CHEESE-CAKE, PLEASE.
UM... IS THAT SIX HUNDWED YEN?
RIGHT. HERE YOU GO.
HUH?
A WITTLE SILVER MONEY
AND A BIG SILVER MONEY?
Buh...
THE BIG ONE IS FIVE TIMES THE VALUE OF THE SMALL ONE.
TANK YOU FOR SHOWING ME SOME-THING SO AMAZING.
You can have it back.
YOU DON'T HAVE TO RETURN IT.
HE TREATED ME TO A SMALL CREAM-PUFF.

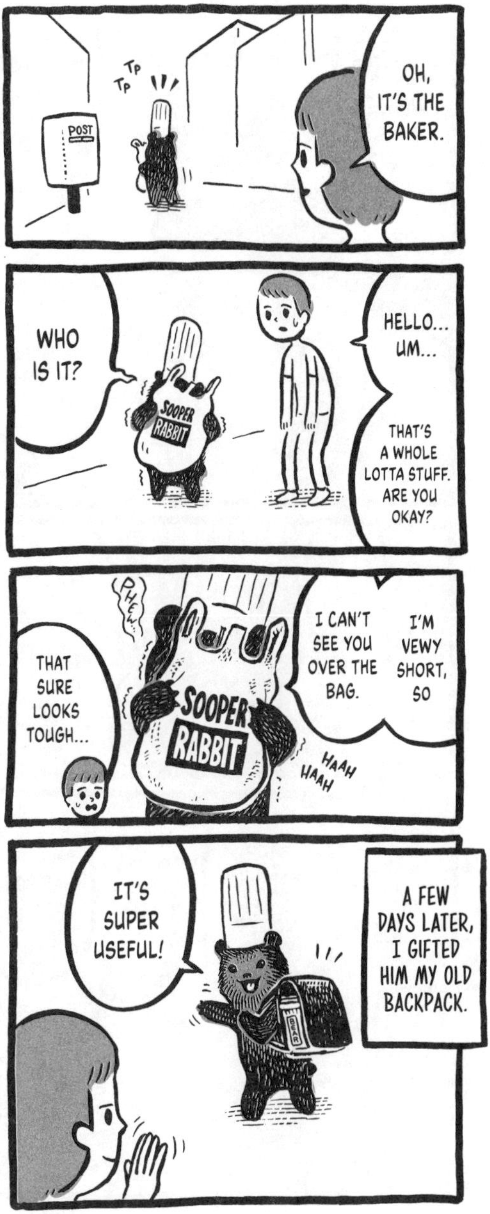
OH, IT'S THE BAKER.
TP TP
POST
HELLO... UM...
THAT'S A WHOLE LOTTA STUFF. ARE YOU OKAY?
WHO IS IT?
SOOPER RABBIT
I'M VEWY SHORT, SO
I CAN'T SEE YOU OVER THE BAG.
HAAH HAAH
SOOPER RABBIT
PHEW
THAT SURE LOOKS TOUGH...
A FEW DAYS LATER, I GIFTED HIM MY OLD BACKPACK.
IT'S SUPER USEFUL!
BEAR

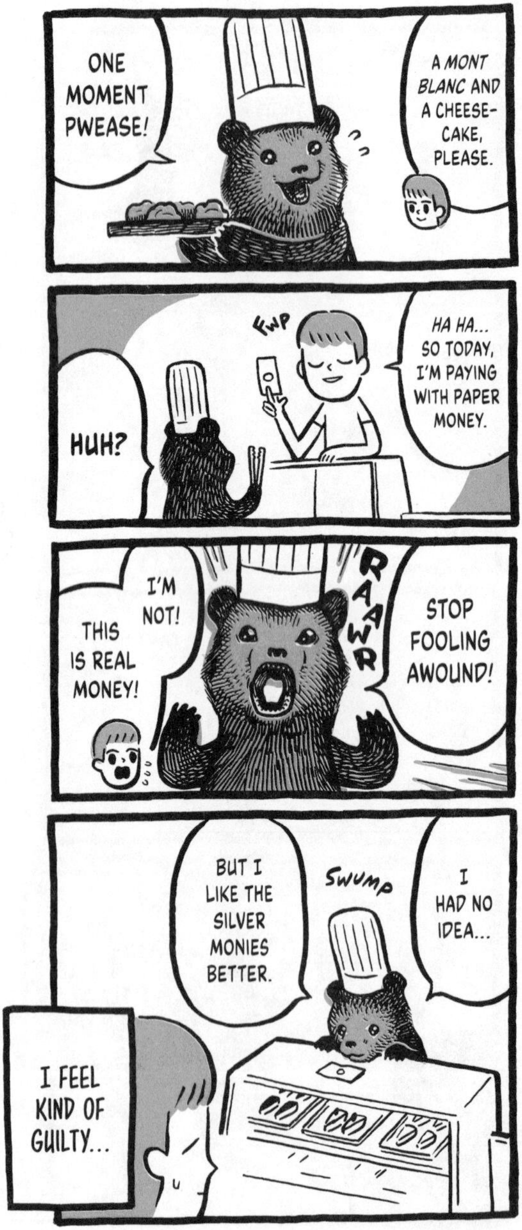
A MONT BLANC AND A CHEESE-CAKE, PLEASE.
ONE MOMENT PWEASE!
HA HA... SO TODAY, I'M PAYING WITH PAPER MONEY.
FWP
HUH?
STOP FOOLING AWOUND!
RAAWR
I'M NOT!
THIS IS REAL MONEY!
I HAD NO IDEA...
SWUMP
BUT I LIKE THE SILVER MONIES BETTER.
I FEEL KIND OF GUILTY...

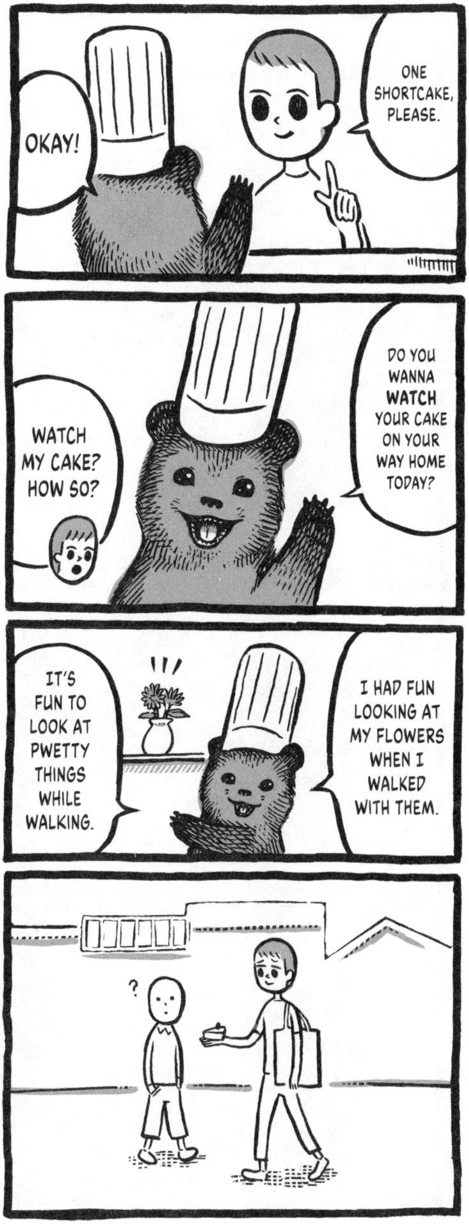
ONE SHORTCAKE, PLEASE.
OKAY!
DO YOU WANNA **WATCH** YOUR CAKE ON YOUR WAY HOME TODAY?
WATCH MY CAKE? HOW SO?
I HAD FUN LOOKING AT MY FLOWERS WHEN I WALKED WITH THEM.
IT'S FUN TO LOOK AT PWETTY THINGS WHILE WALKING.
?

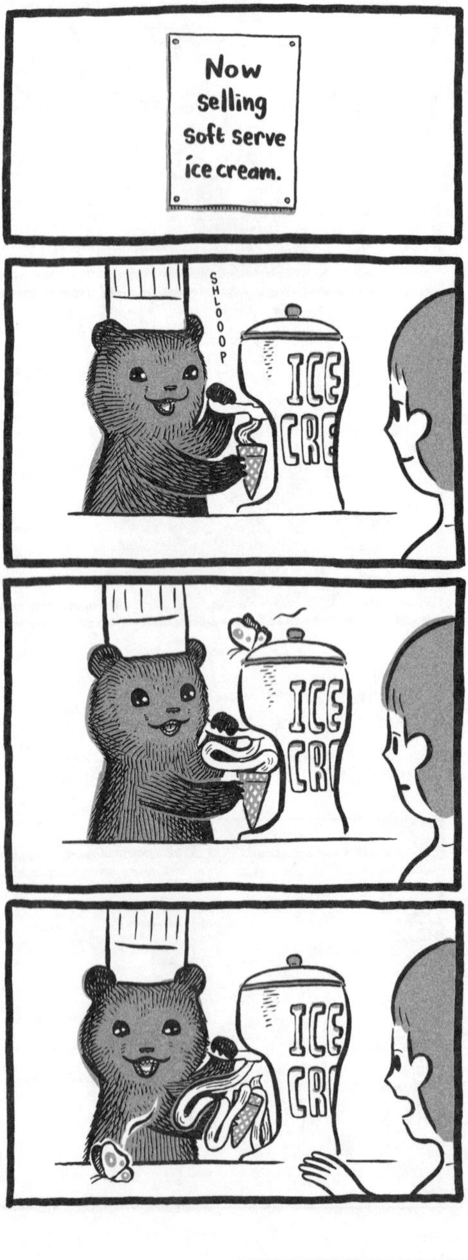
Now selling soft serve ice cream.
SHLOOOP
ICE CRE

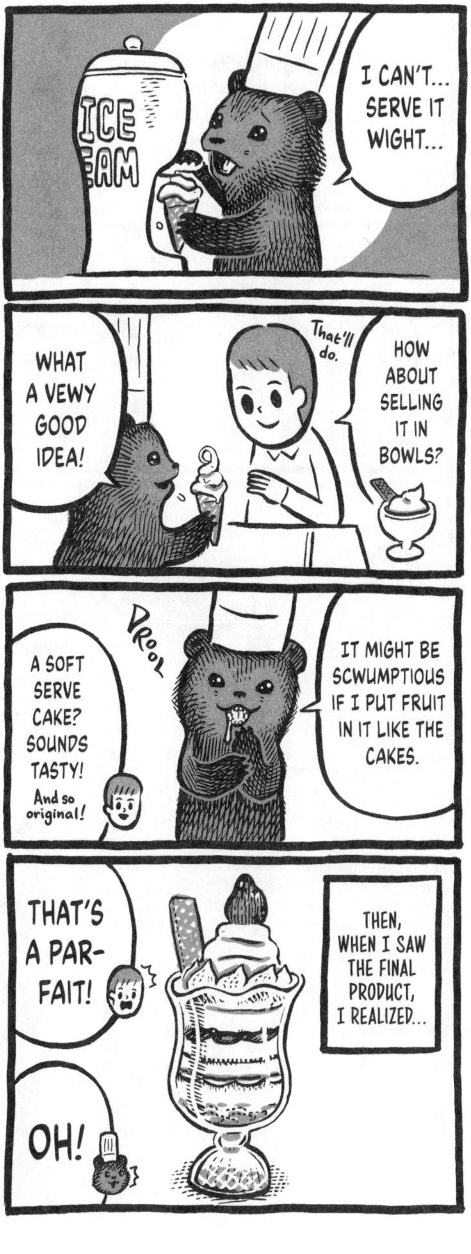
I CAN'T... SERVE IT WIGHT...
HOW ABOUT SELLING IT IN BOWLS?
That'll do.
WHAT A VEWY GOOD IDEA!
IT MIGHT BE SCWUMPTIOUS IF I PUT FRUIT IN IT LIKE THE CAKES.
DROOL
A SOFT SERVE CAKE? SOUNDS TASTY!
And so original!
THEN, WHEN I SAW THE FINAL PRODUCT, I REALIZED...
THAT'S A PAR-FAIT!
OH!

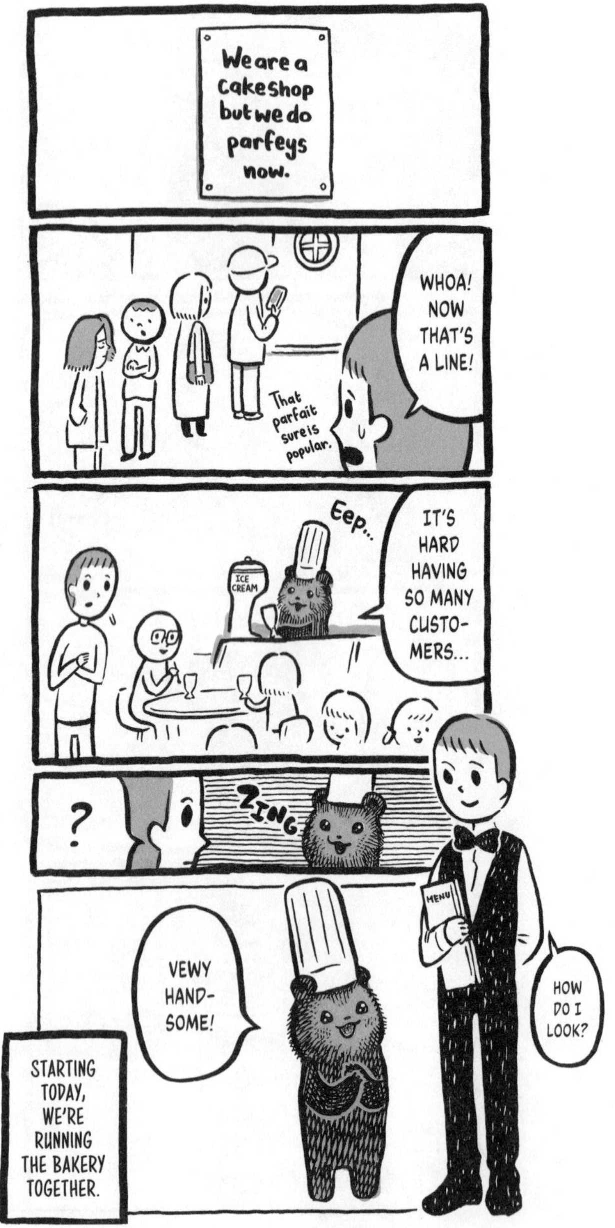
We are a cake shop but we do parfeys now.
WHOA! NOW THAT'S A LINE!
That parfait sure is popular.
IT'S HARD HAVING SO MANY CUSTO-MERS...
Eep...
ICE CREAM
ZING
?
HOW DO I LOOK?
MENU
VEWY HAND-SOME!
STARTING TODAY, WE'RE RUNNING THE BAKERY TOGETHER.

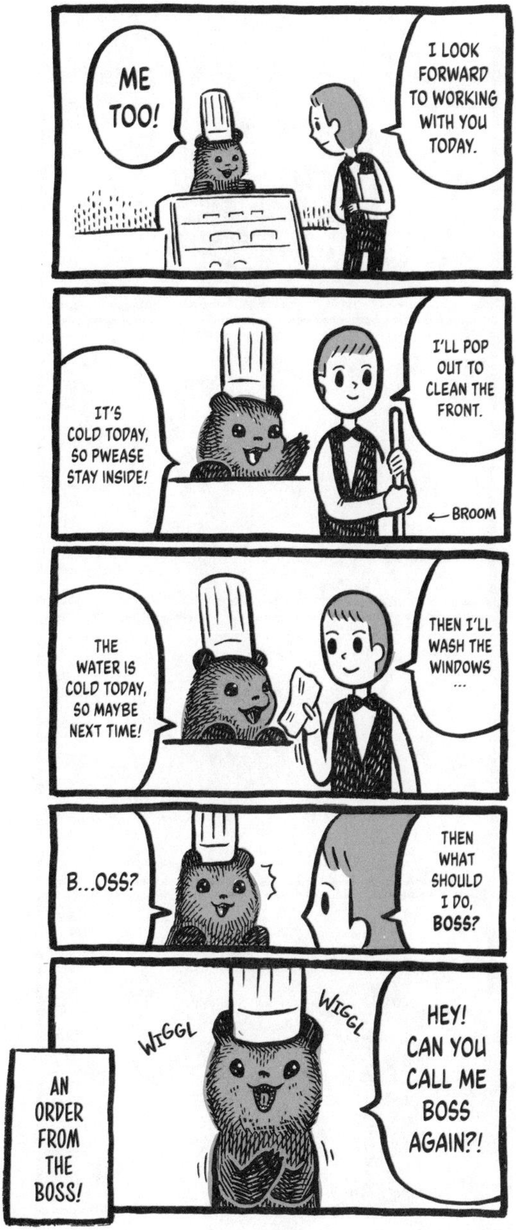
I LOOK FORWARD TO WORKING WITH YOU TODAY.
ME TOO!
I'LL POP OUT TO CLEAN THE FRONT.
IT'S COLD TODAY, SO PWEASE STAY INSIDE!
BROOM
THEN I'LL WASH THE WINDOWS...
THE WATER IS COLD TODAY, SO MAYBE NEXT TIME!
THEN WHAT SHOULD I DO, BOSS?
B...OSS?
HEY! CAN YOU CALL ME BOSS AGAIN?!
WIGGL
WIGGL
AN ORDER FROM THE BOSS!

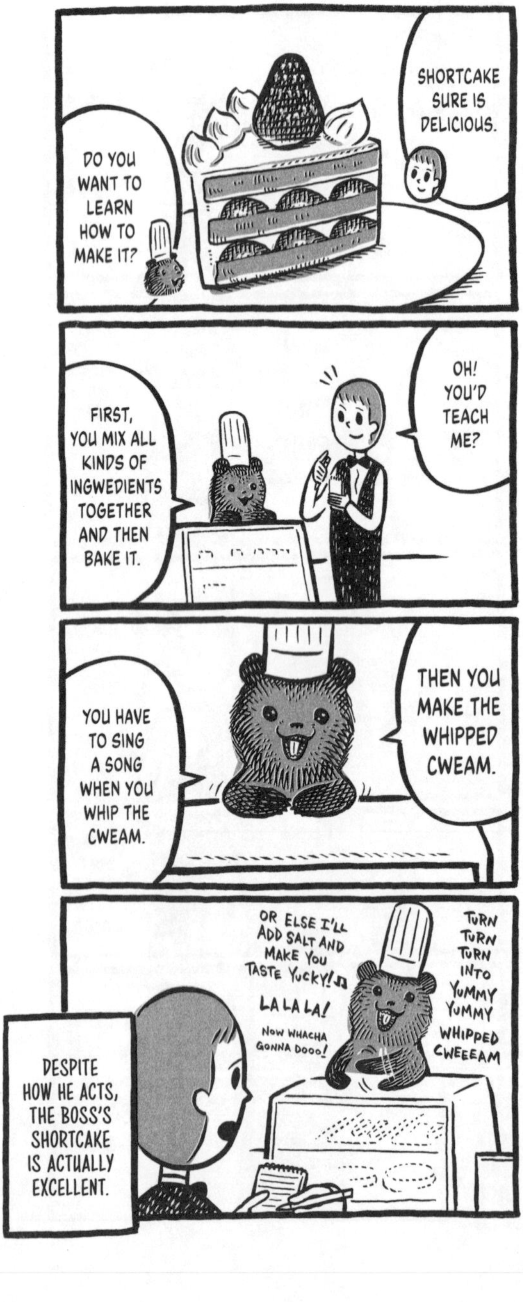
SHORTCAKE SURE IS DELICIOUS.
DO YOU WANT TO LEARN HOW TO MAKE IT?
OH! YOU'D TEACH ME?
FIRST, YOU MIX ALL KINDS OF INGWEDIENTS TOGETHER AND THEN BAKE IT.
THEN YOU MAKE THE WHIPPED CWEAM.
YOU HAVE TO SING A SONG WHEN YOU WHIP THE CWEAM.
TURN TURN TURN INTO YUMMY YUMMY WHIPPED CWEEEAM
OR ELSE I'LL ADD SALT AND MAKE YOU TASTE YUCKY! ♫
LA LA LA!
NOW WHACHA GONNA DOOO!
DESPITE HOW HE ACTS, THE BOSS'S SHORTCAKE IS ACTUALLY EXCELLENT.

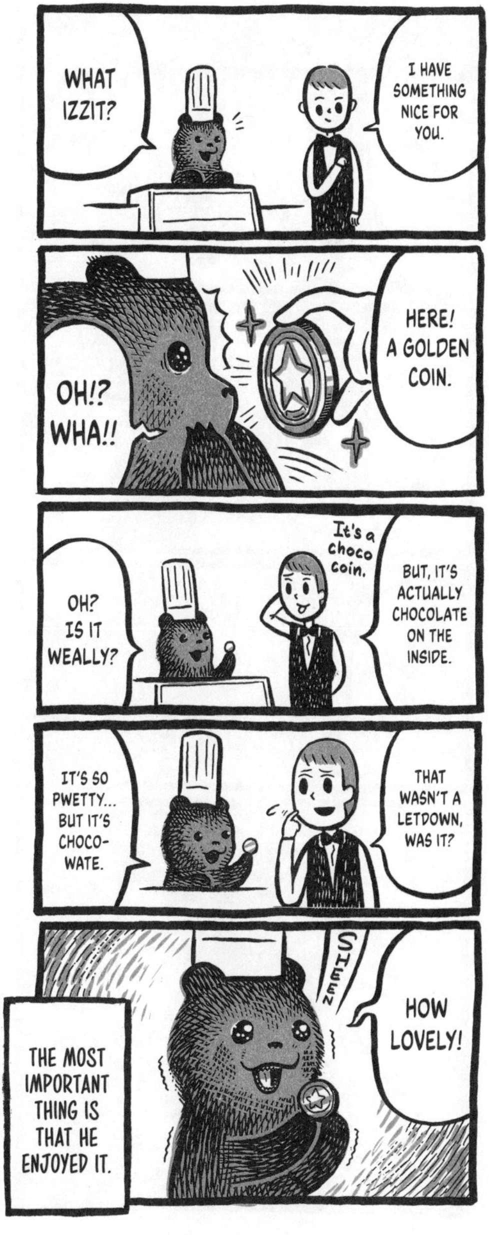
I HAVE SOMETHING NICE FOR YOU.
WHAT IZZIT?
HERE! A GOLDEN COIN.
OH!? WHA!!
BUT, IT'S ACTUALLY CHOCOLATE ON THE INSIDE.
It's a choco coin.
OH? IS IT WEALLY?
THAT WASN'T A LETDOWN, WAS IT?
IT'S SO PWETTY... BUT IT'S CHOCO-WATE.
HOW LOVELY!
SHEEN
THE MOST IMPORTANT THING IS THAT HE ENJOYED IT.

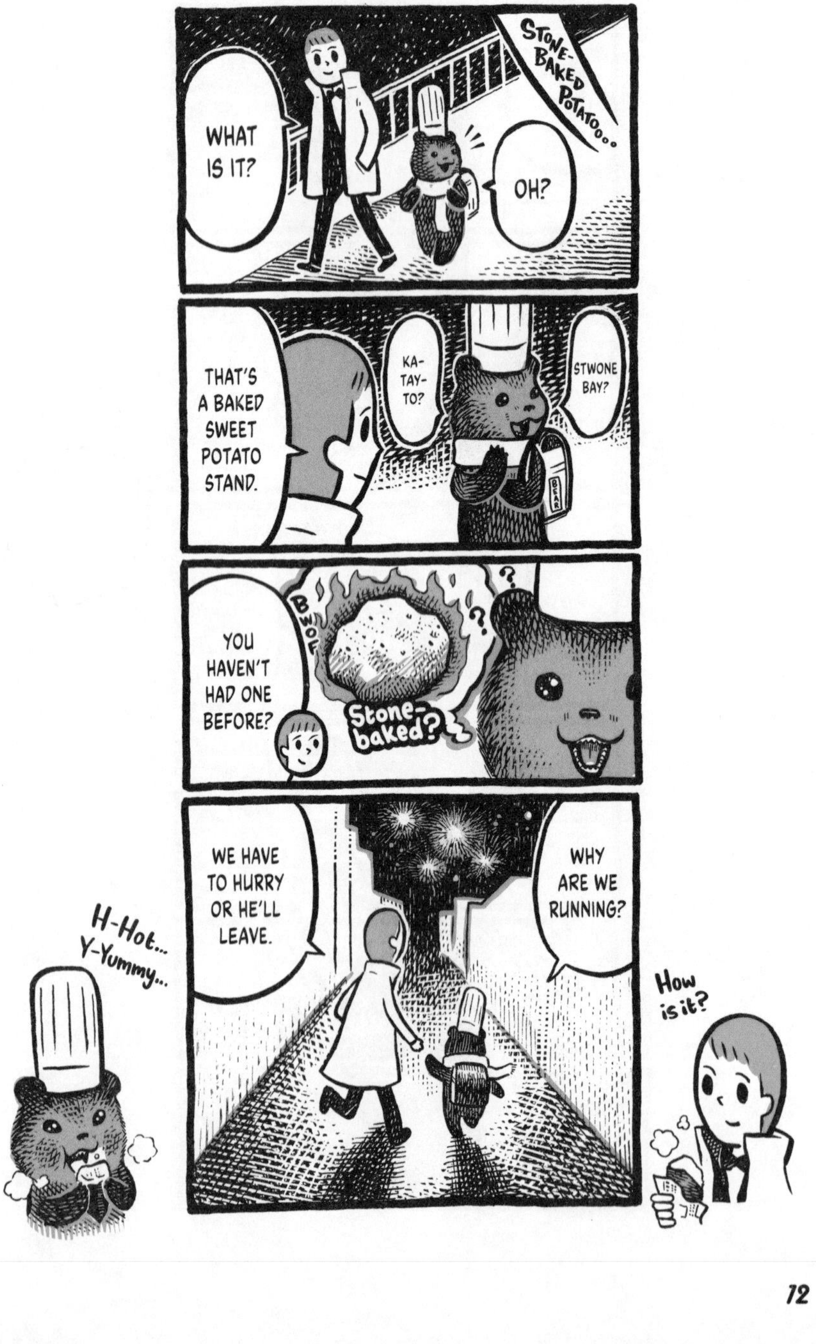
STONE-BAKED POTATOOOO
OH?
WHAT IS IT?
STWONE BAY?
KA-TAY-TO?
THAT'S A BAKED SWEET POTATO STAND.
BEAR
??
BWOF
Stone-baked?
YOU HAVEN'T HAD ONE BEFORE?
WHY ARE WE RUNNING?
WE HAVE TO HURRY OR HE'LL LEAVE.
How is it?
H-Hot... Y-Yummy...

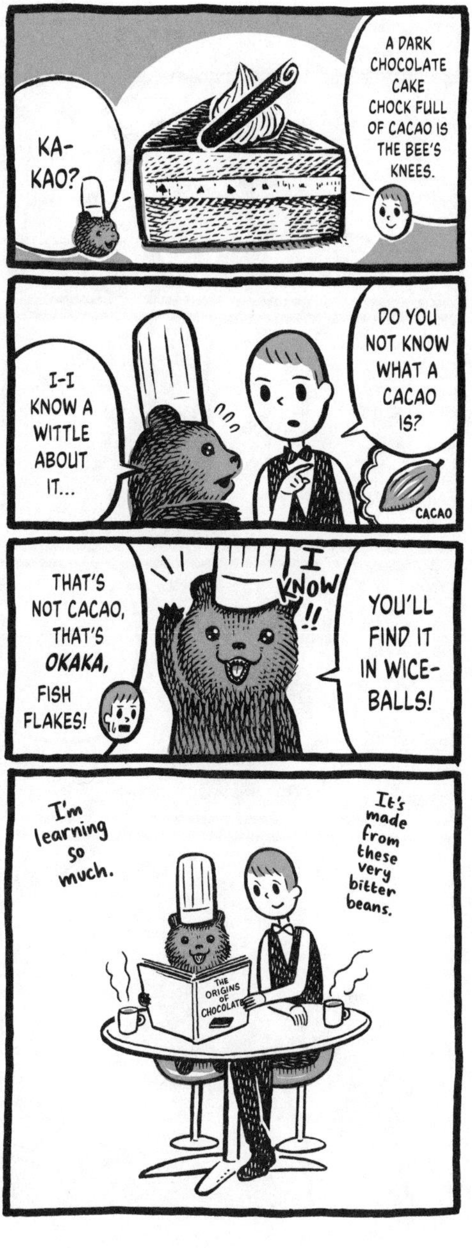
A DARK CHOCOLATE CAKE CHOCK FULL OF CACAO IS THE BEE'S KNEES.
KA-KAO?
DO YOU NOT KNOW WHAT A CACAO IS?
CACAO
I-I KNOW A WITTLE ABOUT IT...
YOU'LL FIND IT IN WICE-BALLS!
I KNOW!!
THAT'S NOT CACAO, THAT'S OKAKA, FISH FLAKES!
It's made from these very bitter beans.
I'm learning so much.
THE ORIGINS OF CHOCOLATE

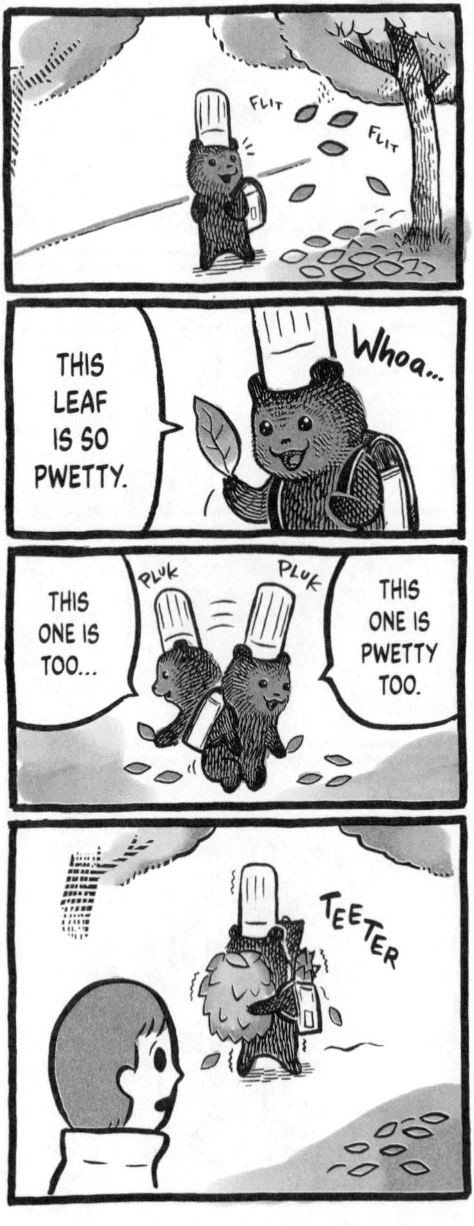
FLIT
FLIT
Whoa...
THIS LEAF IS SO PWETTY.
PLUK
PLUK
THIS ONE IS PWETTY TOO.
THIS ONE IS TOO...
TEETER

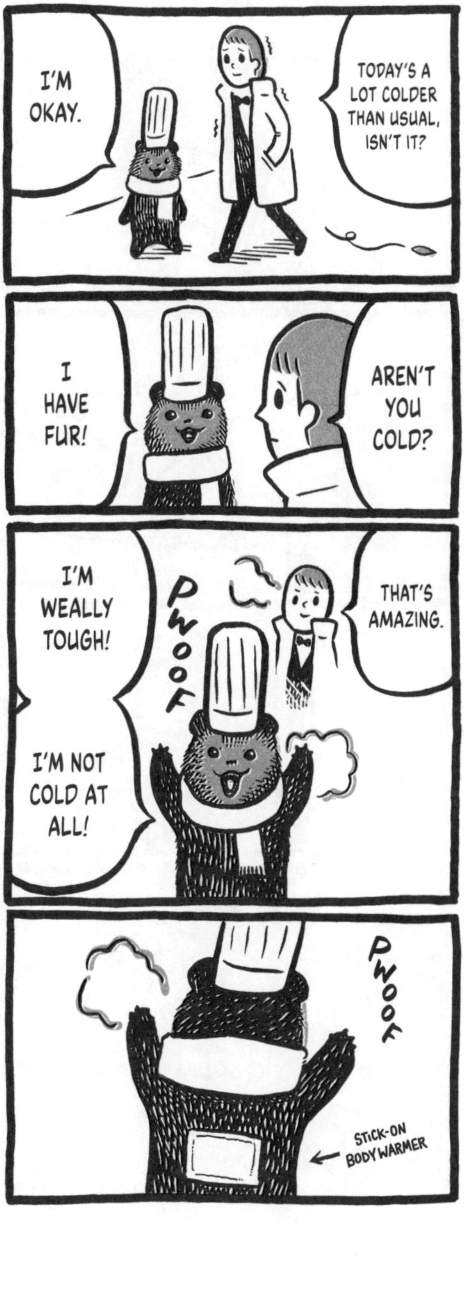
TODAY'S A LOT COLDER THAN USUAL, ISN'T IT?
I'M OKAY.
AREN'T YOU COLD?
I HAVE FUR!
THAT'S AMAZING.
PWOOF
I'M WEALLY TOUGH!
I'M NOT COLD AT ALL!
PWOOF
STICK-ON BODY WARMER

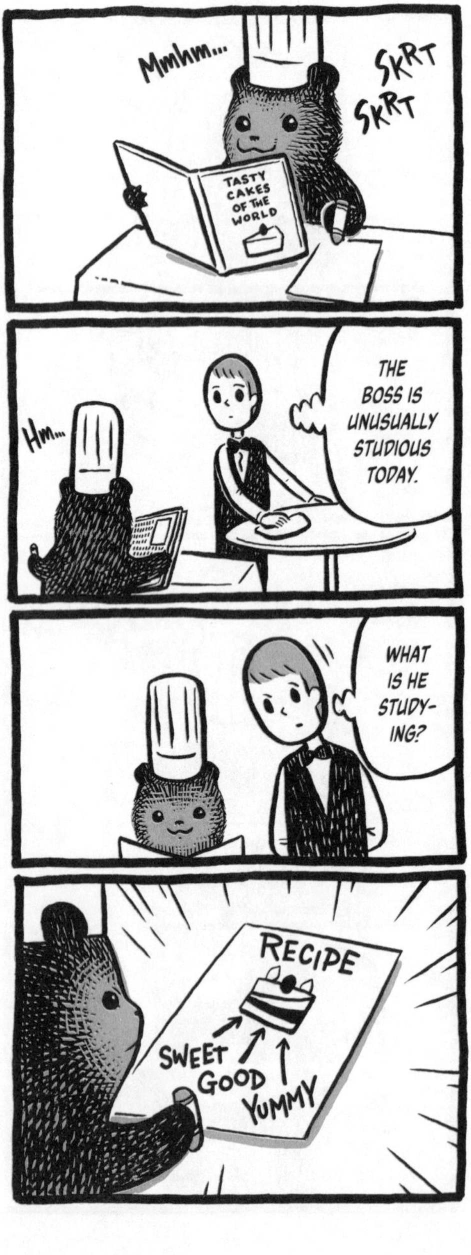
SKRT SKRT
Mmhm...
TASTY CAKES OF THE WORLD
THE BOSS IS UNUSUALLY STUDIOUS TODAY.
Hm...
WHAT IS HE STUDYING?
RECIPE
SWEET
GOOD
YUMMY

HE WAS PRETTY DOWN FOR A WHILE AFTER THAT.

GSHK

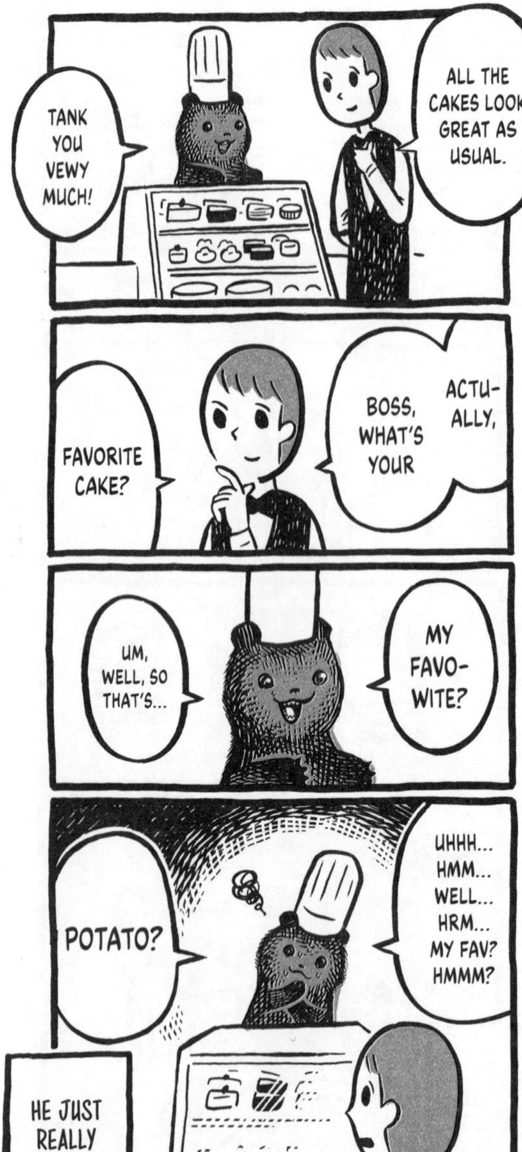
ALL THE CAKES LOOK GREAT AS USUAL.
TANK YOU VEWY MUCH!
ACTU-ALLY, BOSS, WHAT'S YOUR
FAVORITE CAKE?
MY FAVO-WITE?
UM, WELL, SO THAT'S...
UHHH... HMM... WELL... HRM... MY FAV? HMMM?
POTATO?
HE JUST REALLY COULDN'T DECIDE.

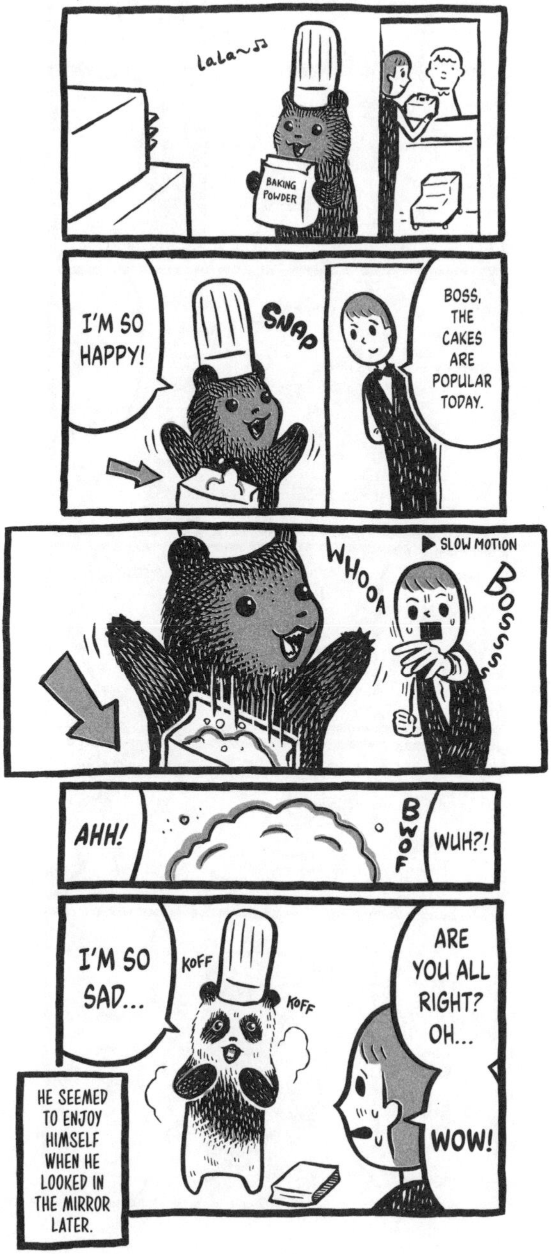
lala~♫
BAKING POWDER
BOSS, THE CAKES ARE POPULAR TODAY.
SNAP
I'M SO HAPPY!
SLOW MOTION
BOSSSSS
WHOOA
WUH?!
BWOF
AHH!
ARE YOU ALL RIGHT? OH...
KOFF
KOFF
I'M SO SAD...
WOW!
HE SEEMED TO ENJOY HIMSELF WHEN HE LOOKED IN THE MIRROR LATER.

Do you get it?

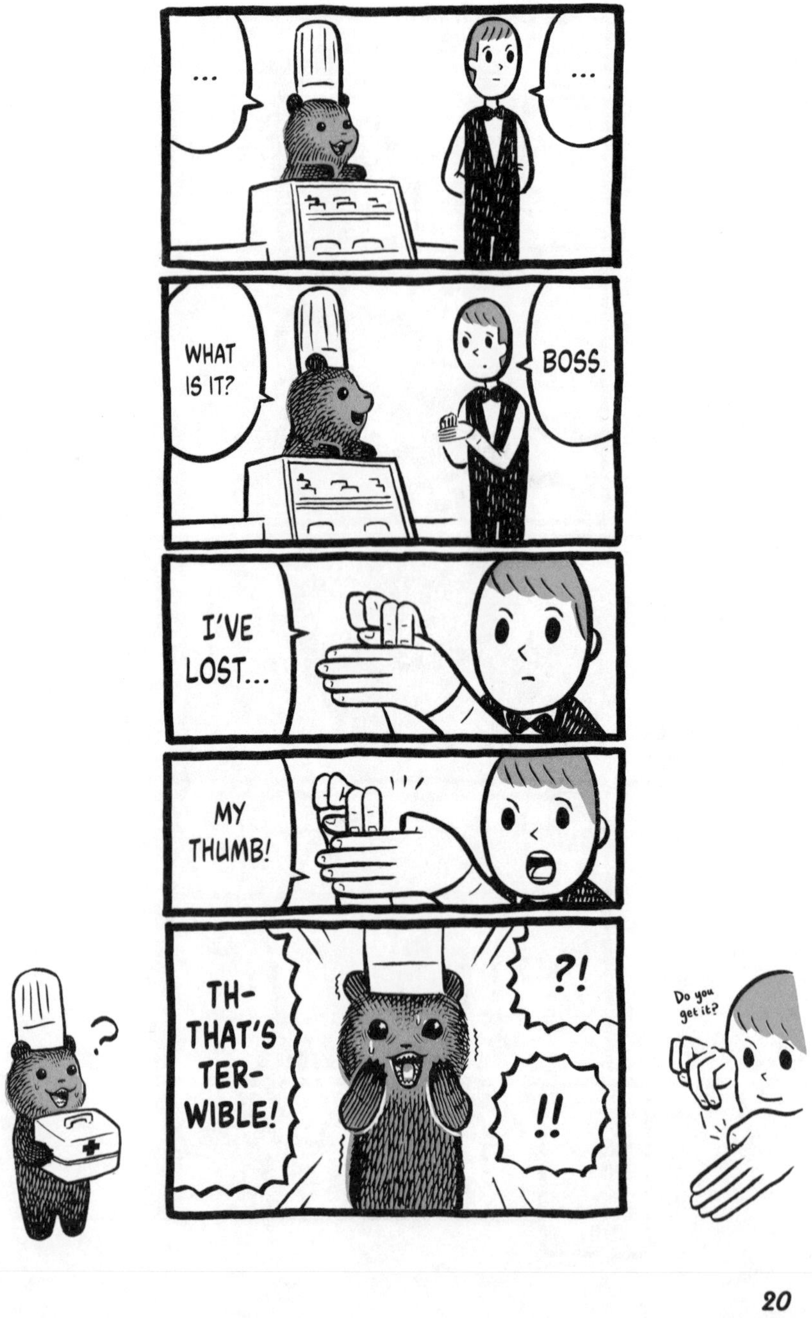
...
...
BOSS.
WHAT IS IT?
I'VE LOST...
MY THUMB!
?!
!!
TH- THAT'S TER- WIBLE!

?

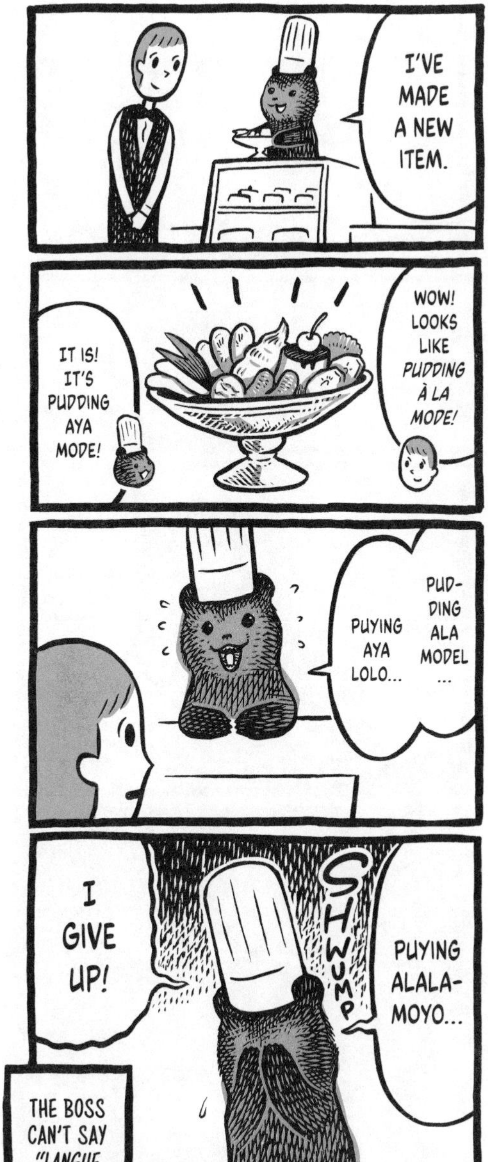
I'VE MADE A NEW ITEM.
WOW! LOOKS LIKE *PUDDING À LA MODE!*
IT IS! IT'S PUDDING AYA MODE!
PUD-DING ALA MODEL ...
PUYING AYA LOLO...
PUYING ALALA-MOYO...
SHWUMP
I GIVE UP!
THE BOSS CAN'T SAY *"LANGUE DE CHAT"* EITHER.

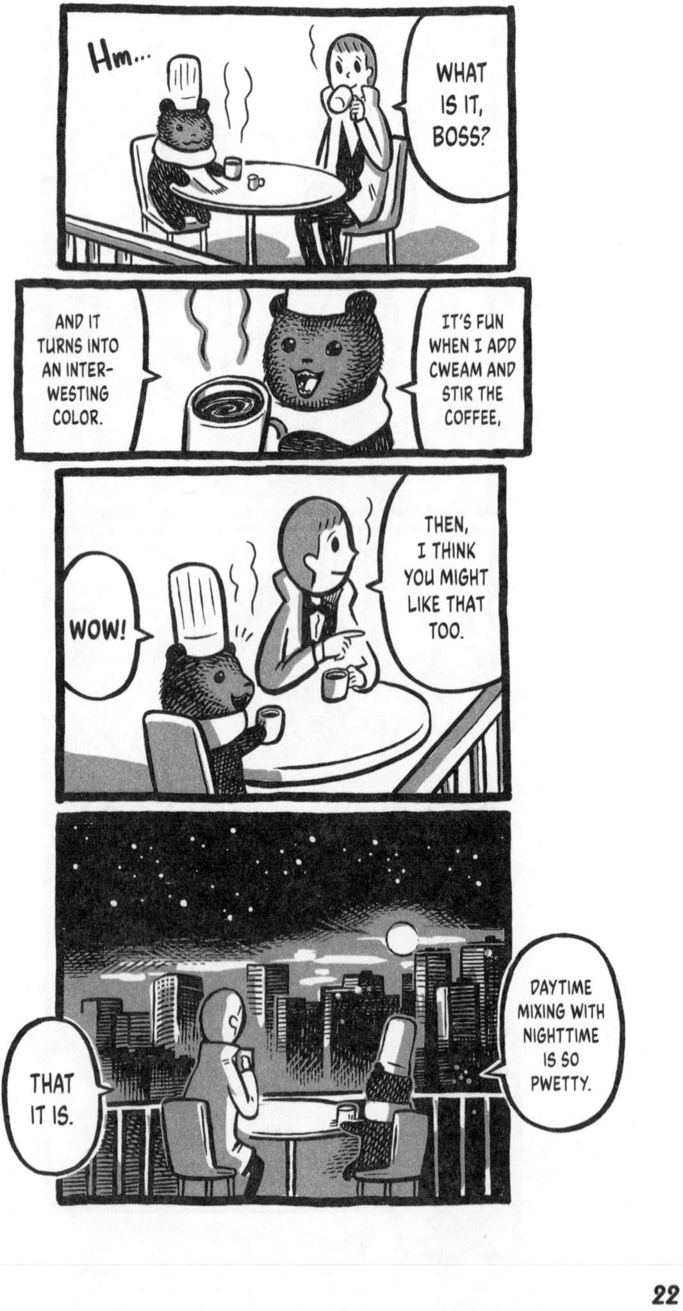
Hm...
WHAT IS IT, BOSS?
IT'S FUN WHEN I ADD CWEAM AND STIR THE COFFEE,
AND IT TURNS INTO AN INTER-WESTING COLOR.
THEN, I THINK YOU MIGHT LIKE THAT TOO.
WOW!
DAYTIME MIXING WITH NIGHTTIME IS SO PWETTY.
THAT IT IS.

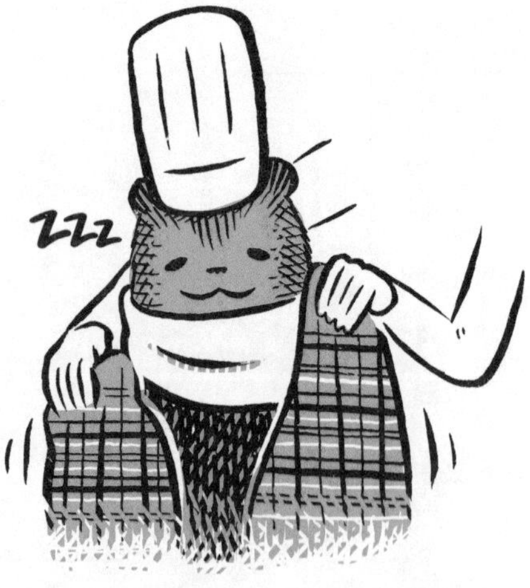
zzz

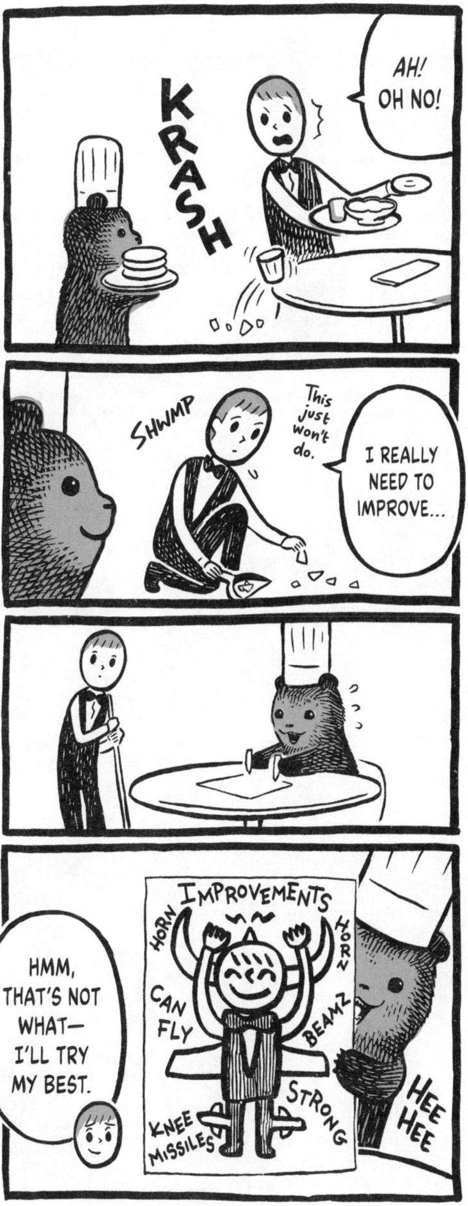
AH! OH NO!
KRASH
This just won't do.
I REALLY NEED TO IMPROVE...
SHWMP
IMPROVEMENTS
HORN
HORN
BEAMZ
CAN FLY
STRONG
KNEE MISSILES
HEE HEE
HMM, THAT'S NOT WHAT— I'LL TRY MY BEST.

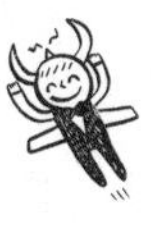

IT'S ALMOST CHRISTMAS, ISN'T IT?
YOU MISS CHRIS?
BOSS, YOU DON'T KNOW ABOUT CHRISTMAS?!
I DON'T WEALLY ...
IT'S THE BUSIEST TIME OF YEAR FOR BAKERIES...
Oh no...
?
IS IT A DAY WHEN YOU EAT CAKE?
YES. PLUS A MAN NAMED SANTA SNEAKS AROUND AT NIGHT
HOHO..
AND PACKS YOUR STOCKINGS WITH PRESENTS.
I'm Mr. San Tah.
WOAH!
Have some gifts.
I'M NOT SURE WHY, BUT HE STARTED SHAKING AFTER THIS.

LOOKING GOOD!!

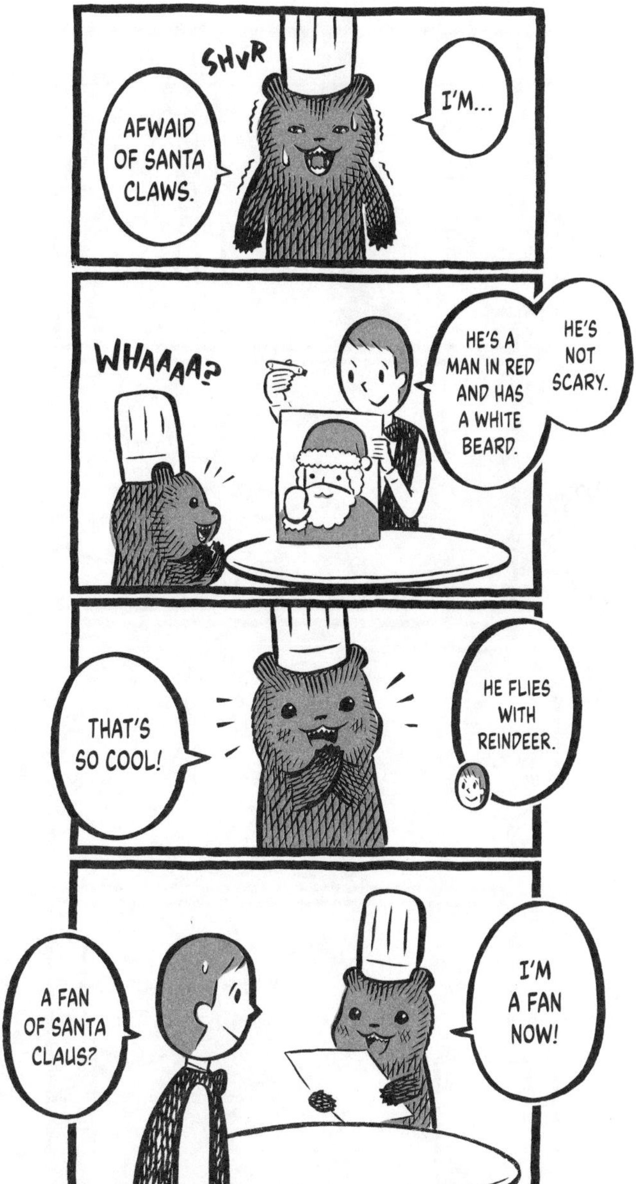
I'M...
SHVR
AFWAID OF SANTA CLAWS.
HE'S NOT SCARY.
HE'S A MAN IN RED AND HAS A WHITE BEARD.
WHAAAA?
HE FLIES WITH REINDEER.
THAT'S SO COOL!
I'M A FAN NOW!
A FAN OF SANTA CLAUS?

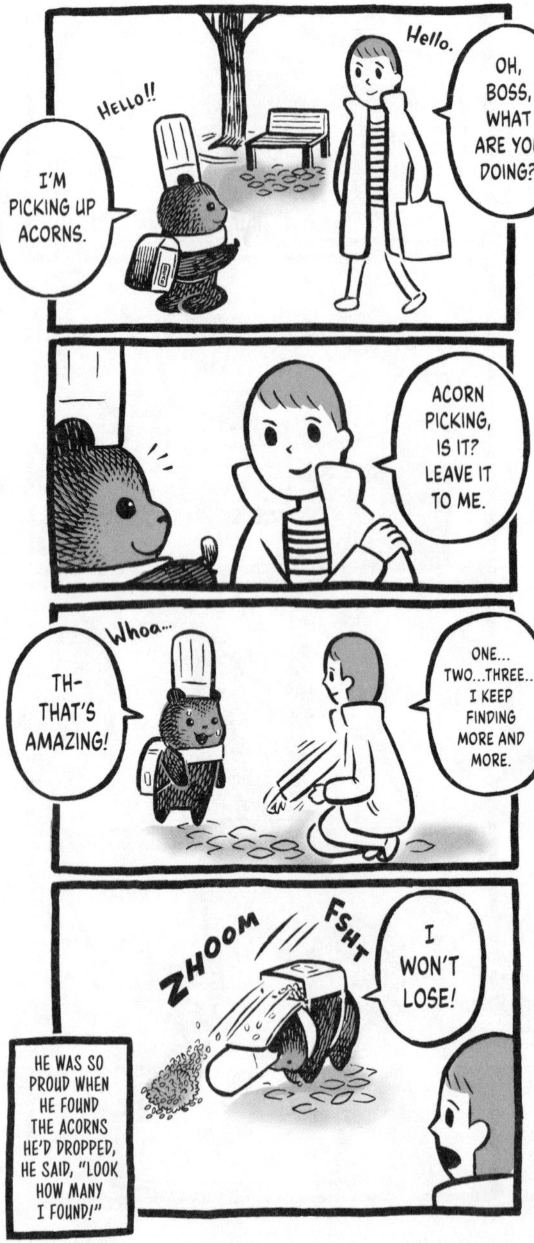

Hello.
OH, BOSS, WHAT ARE YOU DOING?
HELLO!!
I'M PICKING UP ACORNS.
ACORN PICKING, IS IT? LEAVE IT TO ME.
ONE... TWO...THREE... I KEEP FINDING MORE AND MORE.
Whoa...
TH-THAT'S AMAZING!
I WON'T LOSE!
FSHT
ZHOOM
HE WAS SO PROUD WHEN HE FOUND THE ACORNS HE'D DROPPED, HE SAID, "LOOK HOW MANY I FOUND!"

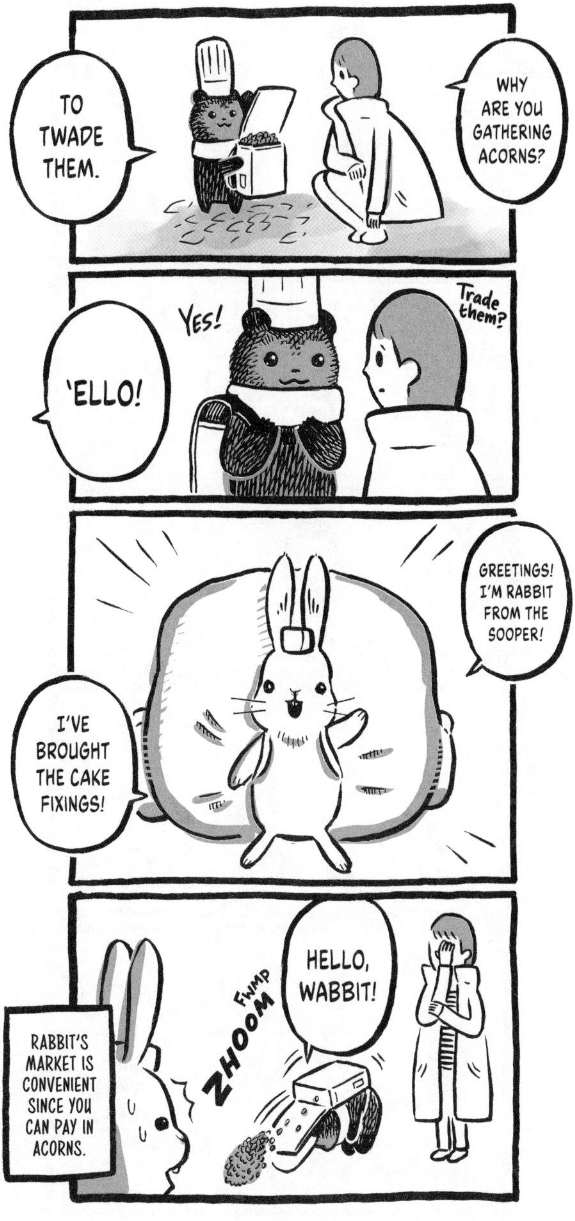
WHY ARE YOU GATHERING ACORNS?
TO TWADE THEM.
Trade them?
YES!
'ELLO!
GREETINGS! I'M RABBIT FROM THE SOOPER!
I'VE BROUGHT THE CAKE FIXINGS!
HELLO, WABBIT!
FWMP
ZHOOM
RABBIT'S MARKET IS CONVENIENT SINCE YOU CAN PAY IN ACORNS.

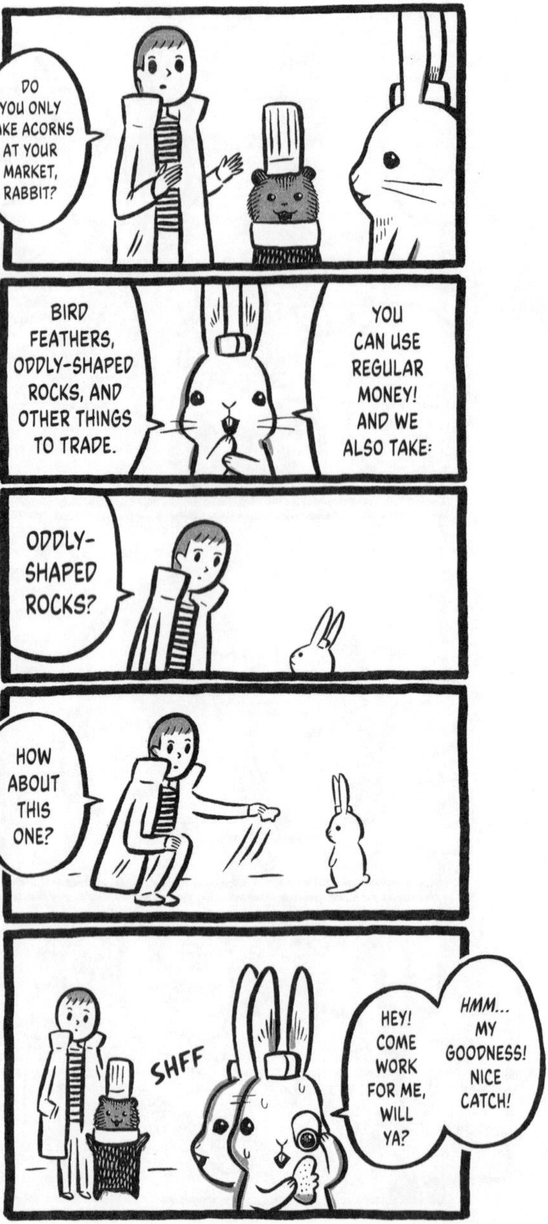
DO YOU ONLY TAKE ACORNS AT YOUR MARKET, RABBIT?
YOU CAN USE REGULAR MONEY! AND WE ALSO TAKE:
BIRD FEATHERS, ODDLY-SHAPED ROCKS, AND OTHER THINGS TO TRADE.
ODDLY-SHAPED ROCKS?
HOW ABOUT THIS ONE?
HMM... MY GOODNESS! NICE CATCH!
HEY! COME WORK FOR ME, WILL YA?
SHFF

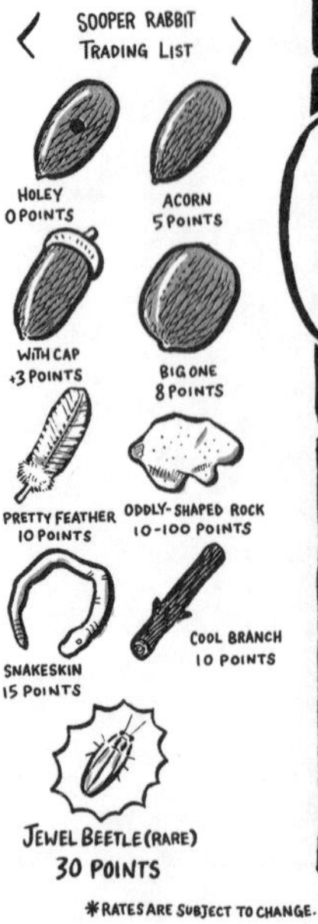
SOOPER RABBIT TRADING LIST
HOLEY 0 POINTS
ACORN 5 POINTS
WITH CAP +3 POINTS
BIG ONE 8 POINTS
PRETTY FEATHER 10 POINTS
ODDLY-SHAPED ROCK 10-100 POINTS
SNAKESKIN 15 POINTS
COOL BRANCH 10 POINTS
JEWEL BEETLE (RARE) 30 POINTS
*RATES ARE SUBJECT TO CHANGE.

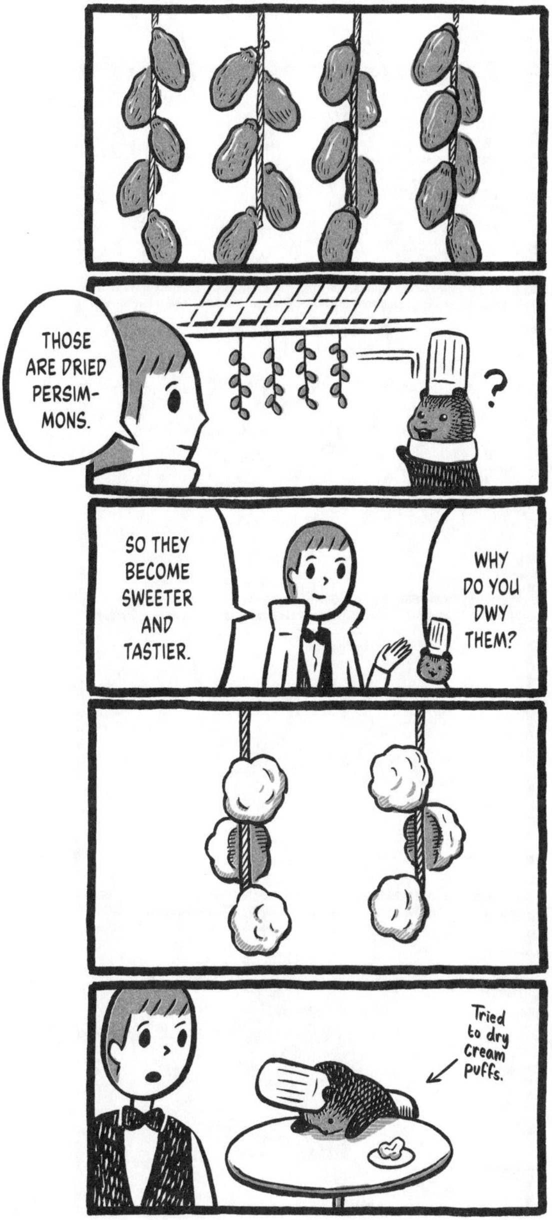
THOSE ARE DRIED PERSIM-MONS.
WHY DO YOU DWY THEM?
SO THEY BECOME SWEETER AND TASTIER.
Tried to dry cream puffs.

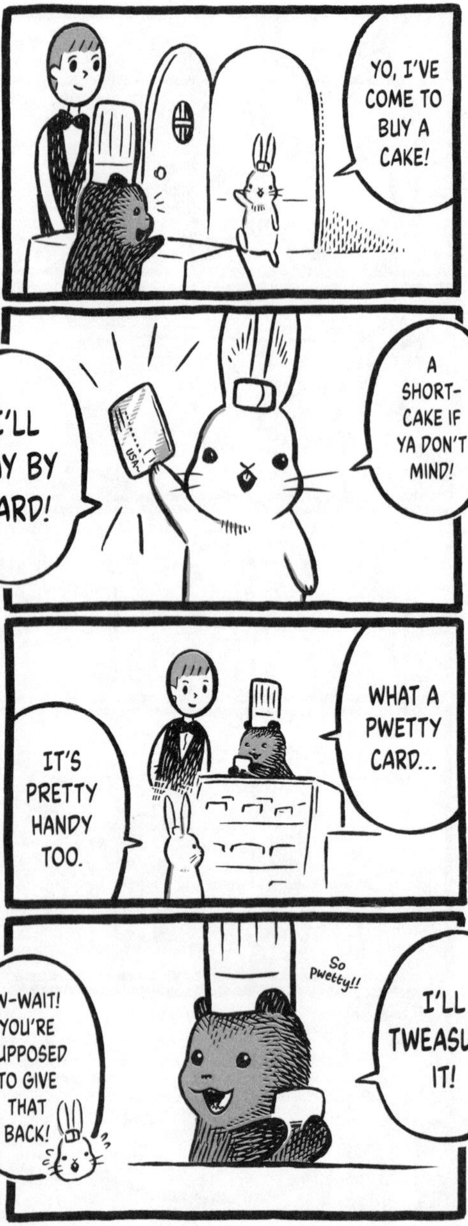
YO, I'VE COME TO BUY A CAKE!
A SHORT-CAKE IF YA DON'T MIND!
I'LL PAY BY CARD!
USA
WHAT A PWETTY CARD...
IT'S PRETTY HANDY TOO.
I'LL TWEASURE IT!
So Pwetty!!
W-WAIT! YOU'RE SUPPOSED TO GIVE THAT BACK!

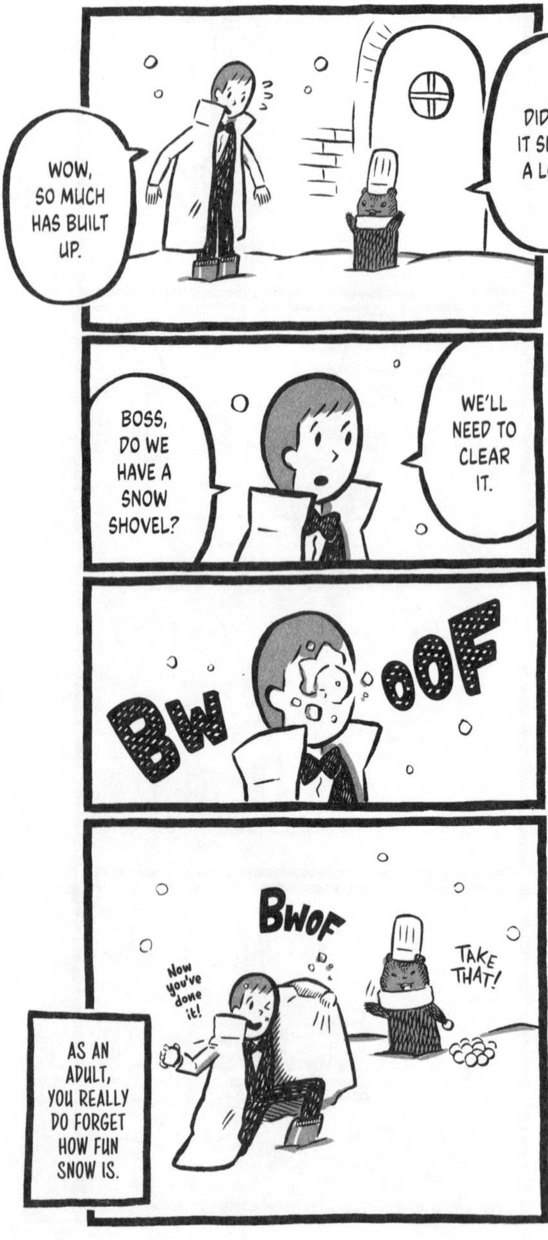
DIDN'T IT SNOW A LOT?
WOW, SO MUCH HAS BUILT UP.
WE'LL NEED TO CLEAR IT.
BOSS, DO WE HAVE A SNOW SHOVEL?
BW OOF
TAKE THAT!
BWOF
Now you've done it!
AS AN ADULT, YOU REALLY DO FORGET HOW FUN SNOW IS.

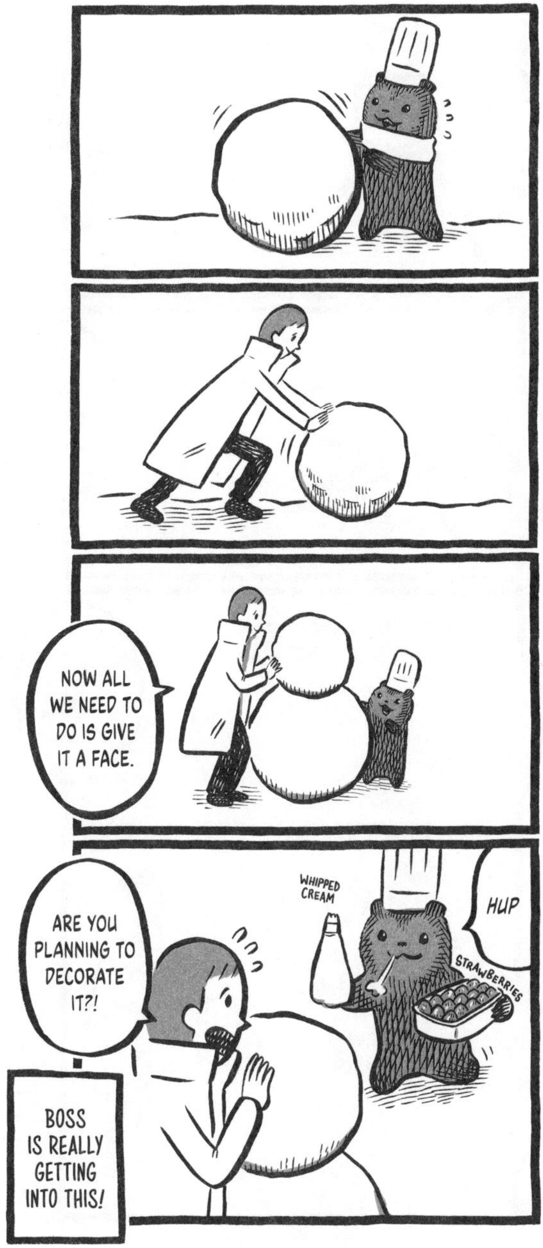
NOW ALL WE NEED TO DO IS GIVE IT A FACE.
HUP
WHIPPED CREAM
STRAWBERRIES
ARE YOU PLANNING TO DECORATE IT?!
BOSS IS REALLY GETTING INTO THIS!

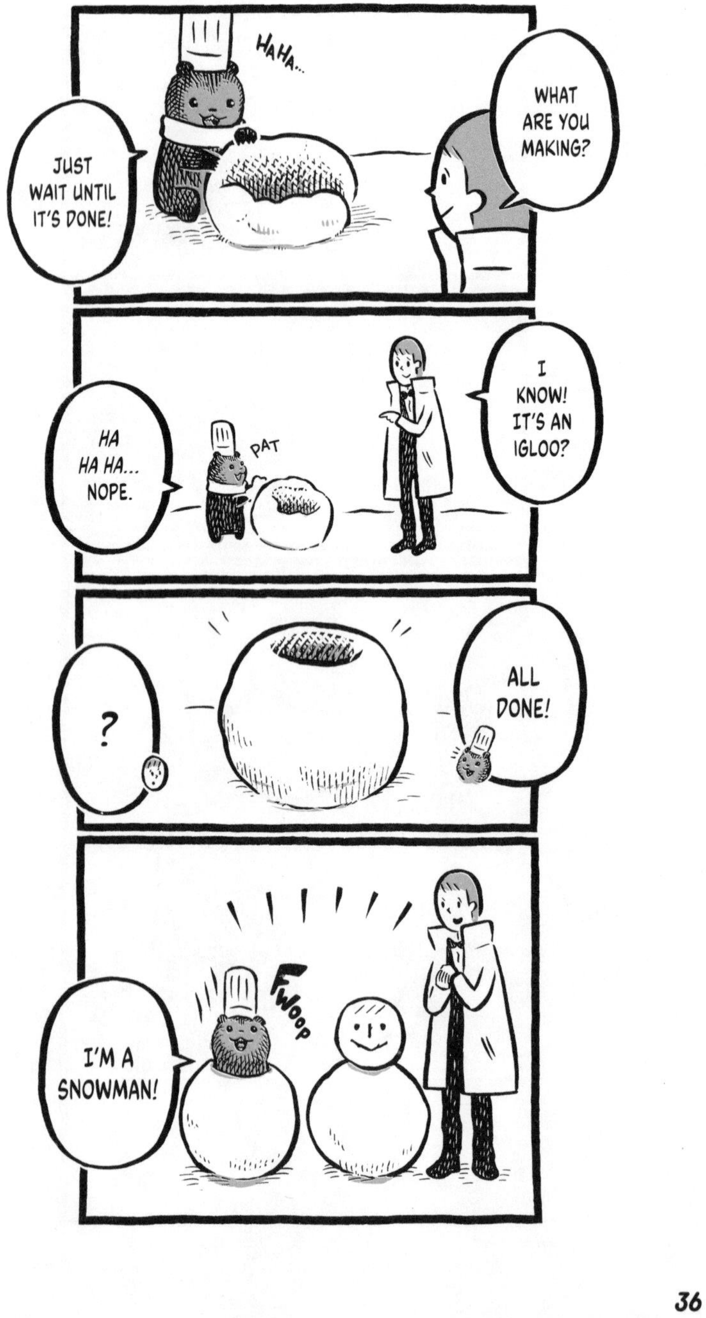
WHAT ARE YOU MAKING?
HAHA...
JUST WAIT UNTIL IT'S DONE!
I KNOW! IT'S AN IGLOO?
PAT
HA HA HA... NOPE.
ALL DONE!
?
FWOOP
I'M A SNOWMAN!

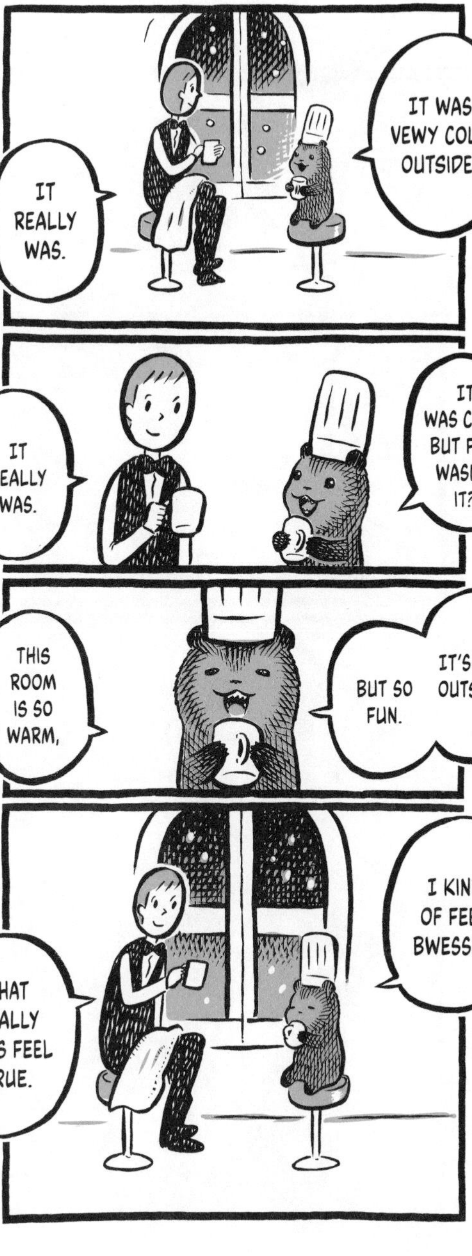
IT WAS VEWY COLD OUTSIDE.
IT REALLY WAS.
IT WAS COLD, BUT FUN, WASN'T IT?
IT REALLY WAS.
IT'S COLD OUTSHIDE,
BUT SO FUN.
THIS ROOM IS SO WARM,
I KIND OF FEEL BWESSED.
THAT REALLY DOES FEEL TRUE.

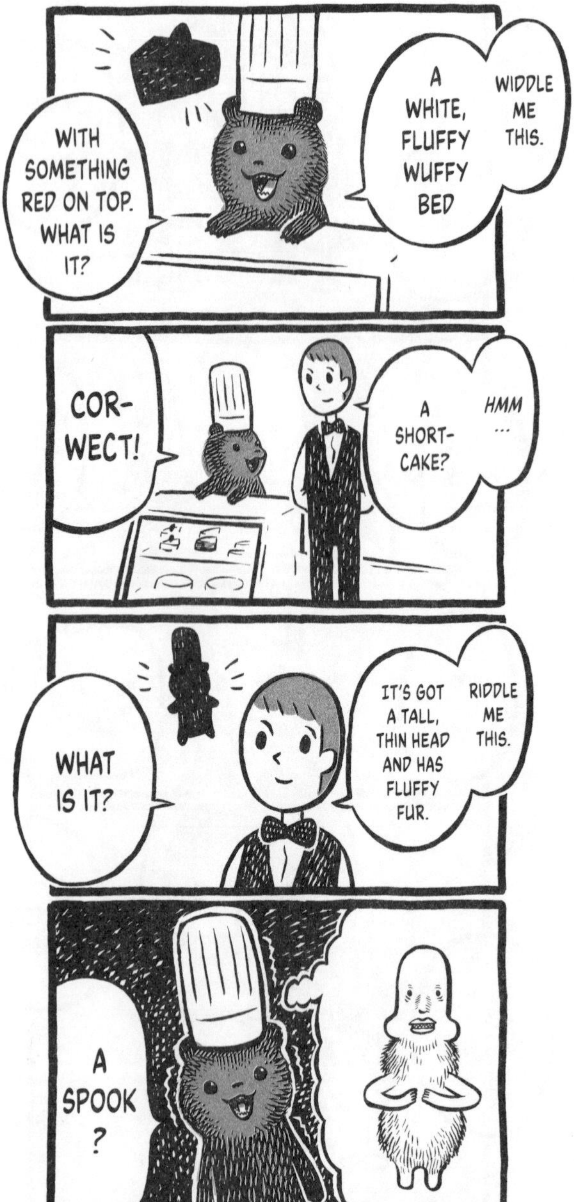
WIDDLE ME THIS.
A WHITE, FLUFFY WUFFY BED
WITH SOMETHING RED ON TOP. WHAT IS IT?
HMM ...
A SHORT-CAKE?
COR-WECT!
RIDDLE ME THIS.
IT'S GOT A TALL, THIN HEAD AND HAS FLUFFY FUR.
WHAT IS IT?
A SPOOK ?

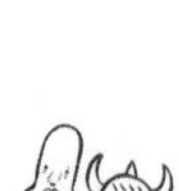

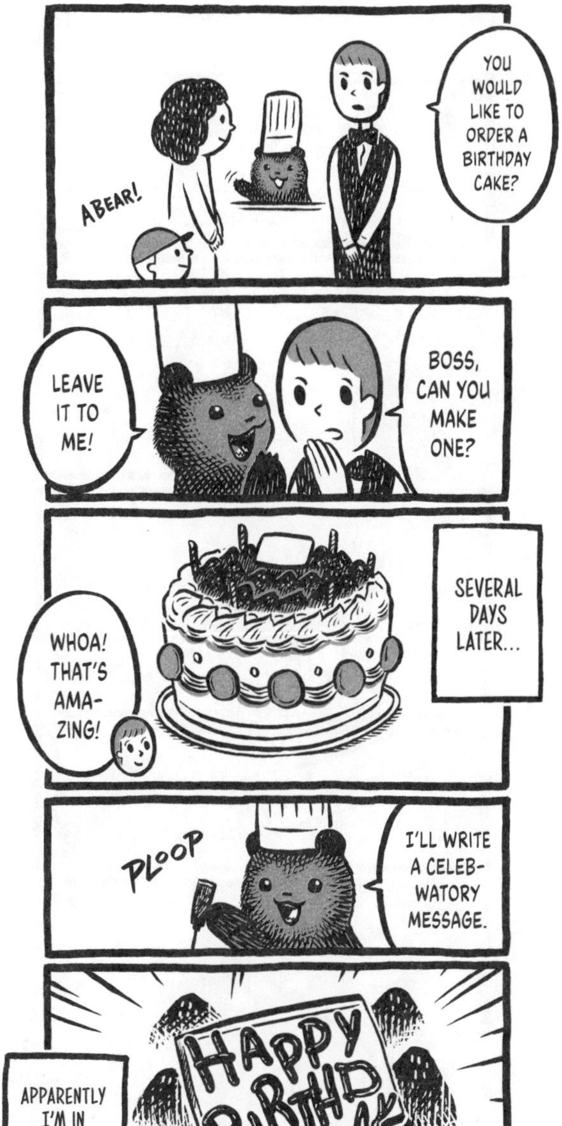
YOU WOULD LIKE TO ORDER A BIRTHDAY CAKE?
A BEAR!
BOSS, CAN YOU MAKE ONE?
LEAVE IT TO ME!
SEVERAL DAYS LATER...
WHOA! THAT'S AMAZING!
I'LL WRITE A CELEBWATORY MESSAGE.
PLOOP
HAPPY BIRTHDAY
APPARENTLY I'M IN CHARGE OF THE FINISHING TOUCHES FROM NOW ON.

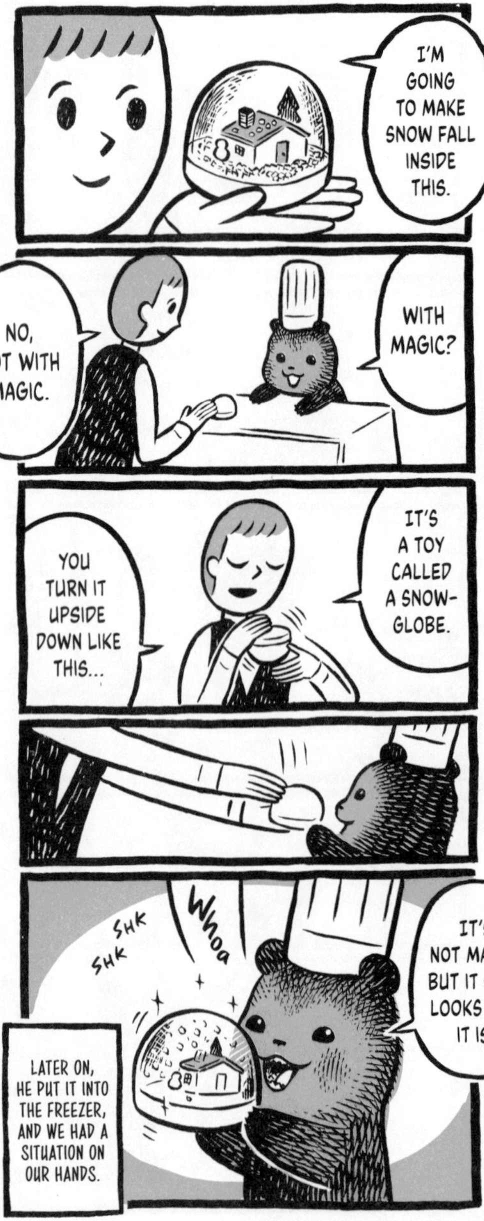
I'M GOING TO MAKE SNOW FALL INSIDE THIS.
WITH MAGIC?
NO, NOT WITH MAGIC.
IT'S A TOY CALLED A SNOW-GLOBE.
YOU TURN IT UPSIDE DOWN LIKE THIS...
IT'S NOT MAGIC, BUT IT SURE LOOKS LIKE IT IS!
Whoa
SHK SHK
LATER ON, HE PUT IT INTO THE FREEZER, AND WE HAD A SITUATION ON OUR HANDS.

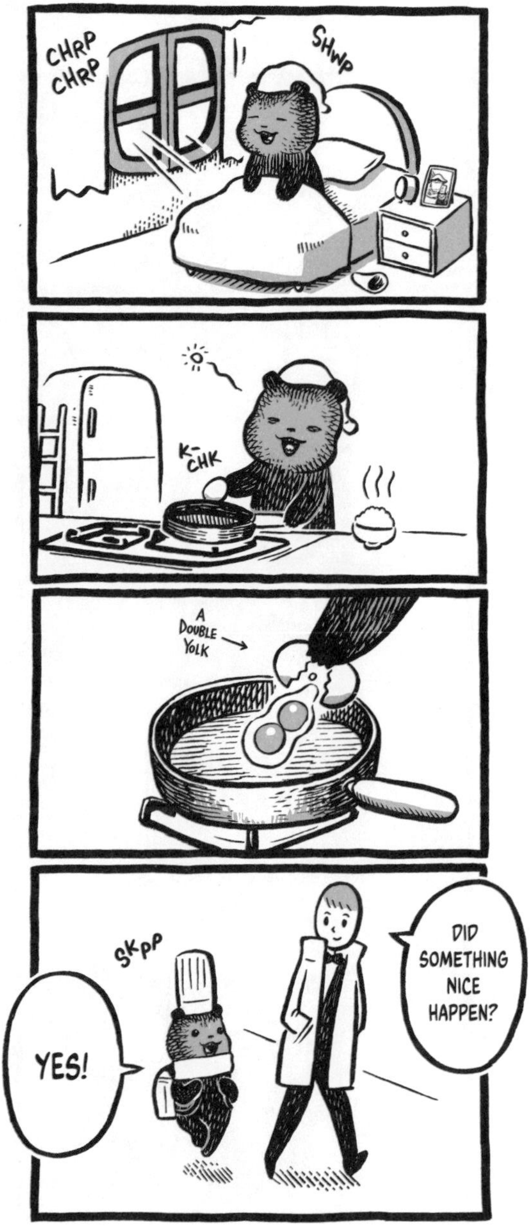
CHRP CHRP
SHWP
K-CHK
A DOUBLE YOLK
DID SOMETHING NICE HAPPEN?
SKPP
YES!

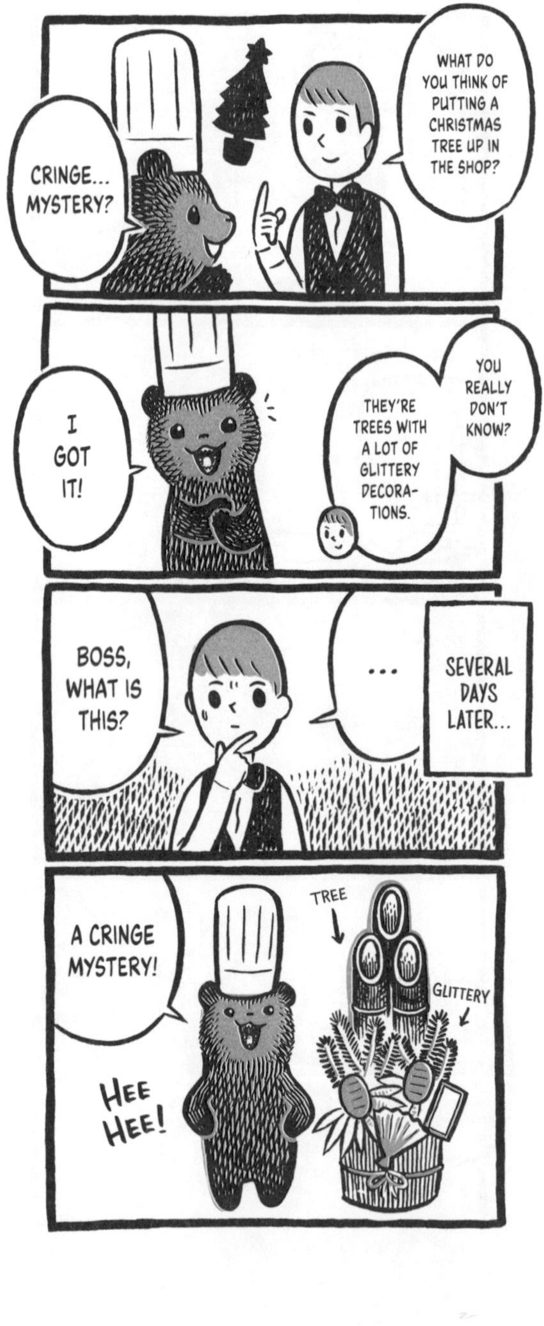
WHAT DO YOU THINK OF PUTTING A CHRISTMAS TREE UP IN THE SHOP?
CRINGE... MYSTERY?
YOU REALLY DON'T KNOW?
THEY'RE TREES WITH A LOT OF GLITTERY DECORA-TIONS.
I GOT IT!
SEVERAL DAYS LATER...
...
BOSS, WHAT IS THIS?
TREE
GLITTERY
A CRINGE MYSTERY!
HEE HEE!

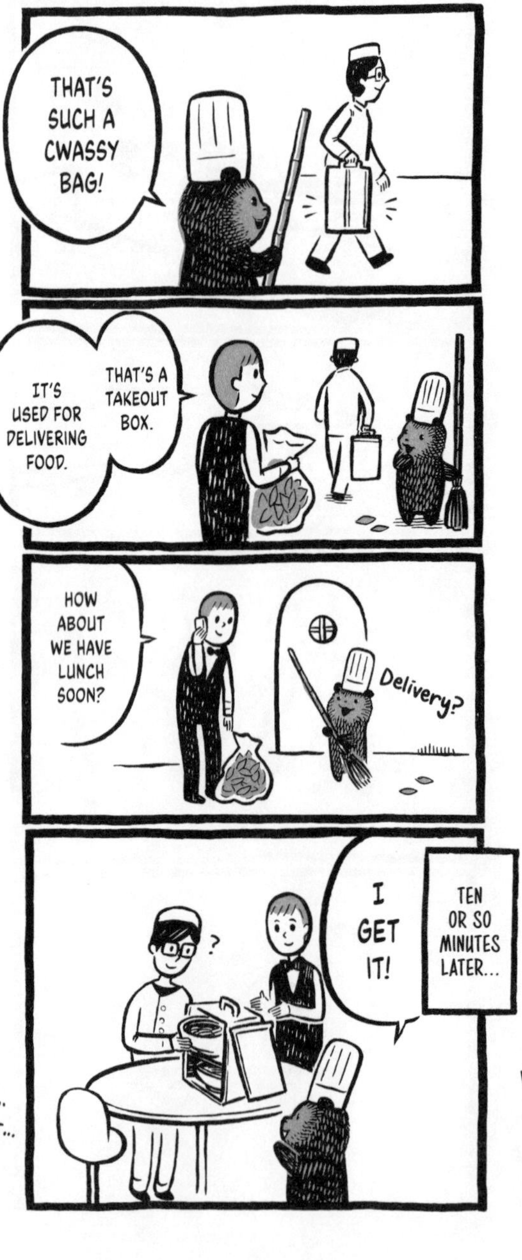
THAT'S SUCH A CWASSY BAG!
THAT'S A TAKEOUT BOX.
IT'S USED FOR DELIVERING FOOD.
HOW ABOUT WE HAVE LUNCH SOON?
Delivery?
TEN OR SO MINUTES LATER...
I GET IT!
?
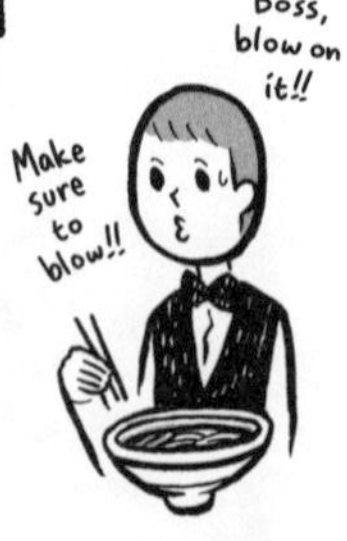
Boss, blow on it!!
Make sure to blow!!
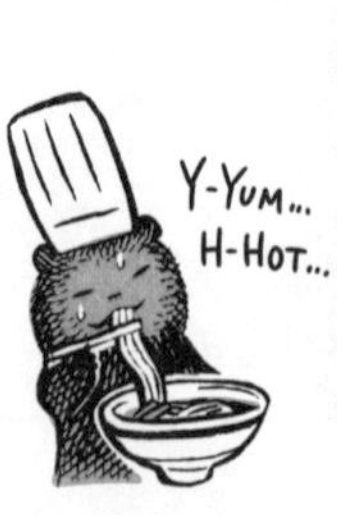
Y-YUM... H-HOT...

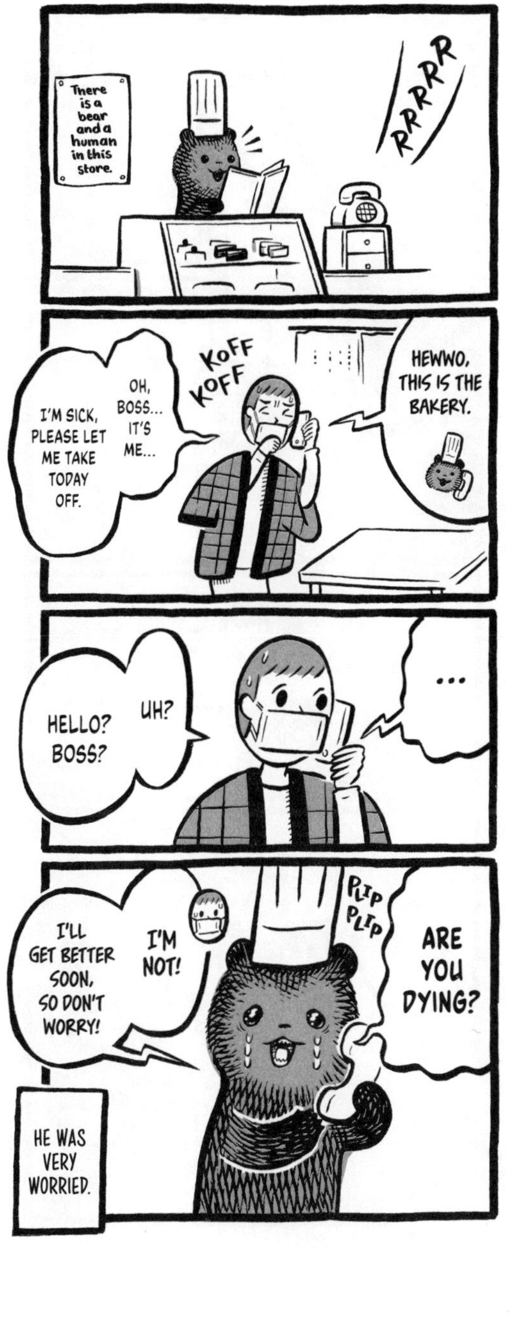
RRRRR
There is a bear and a human in this store.
HEWWO, THIS IS THE BAKERY.
KOFF KOFF
OH, BOSS... IT'S ME...
I'M SICK, PLEASE LET ME TAKE TODAY OFF.
...
UH?
HELLO? BOSS?
ARE YOU DYING?
PLIP PLIP
I'M NOT!
I'LL GET BETTER SOON, SO DON'T WORRY!
HE WAS VERY WORRIED.

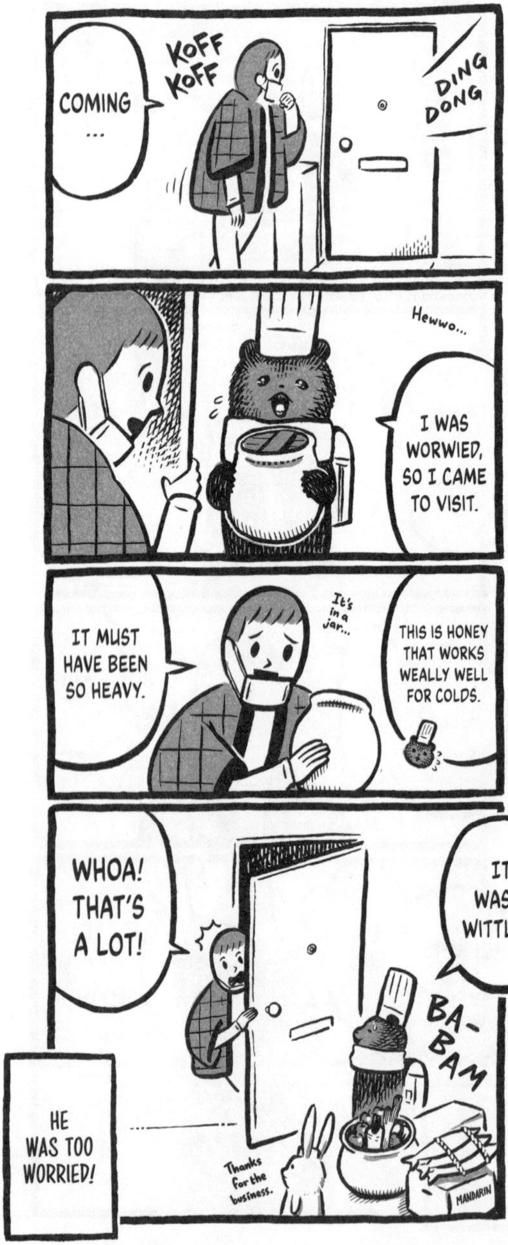
DING DONG
KOFF KOFF
COMING ...
Hewwo...
I WAS WORWIED, SO I CAME TO VISIT.
THIS IS HONEY THAT WORKS WEALLY WELL FOR COLDS.
It's in a jar...
IT MUST HAVE BEEN SO HEAVY.
IT WAS A WITTLE...
BA-BAM
WHOA! THAT'S A LOT!
MANDARIN
Thanks for the business.
HE WAS TOO WORRIED!

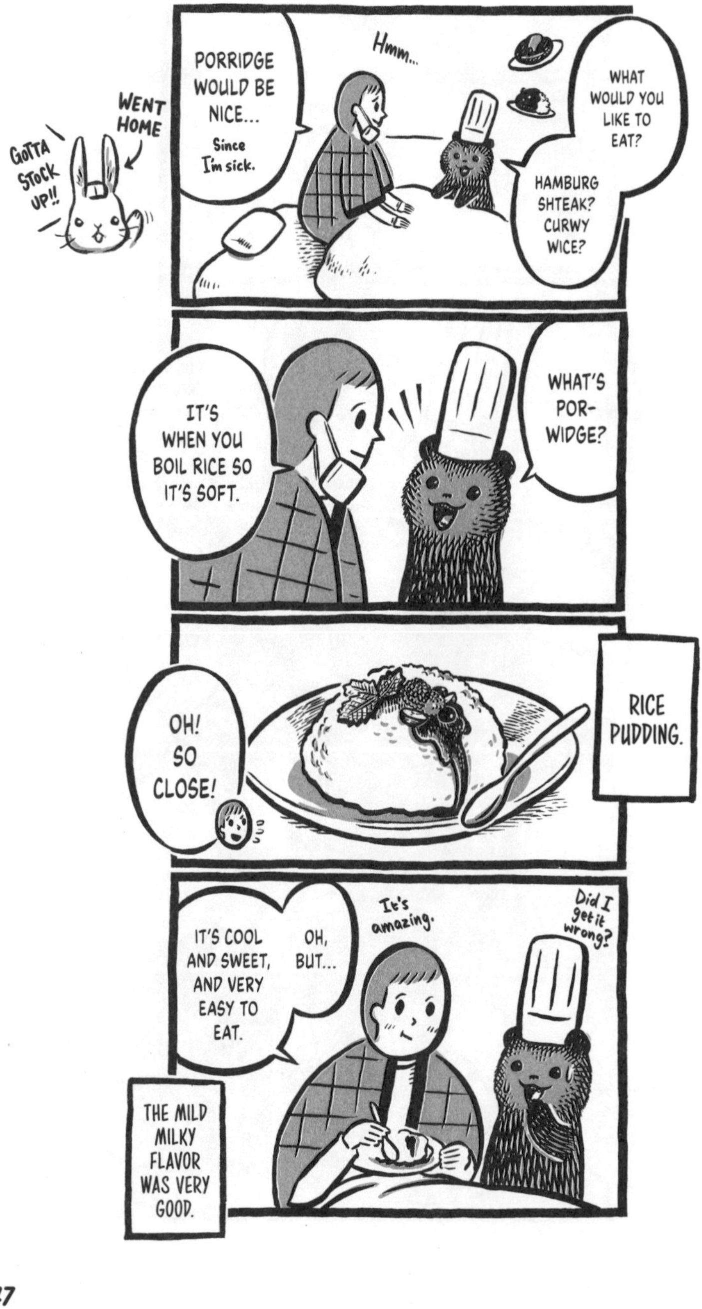
WHAT WOULD YOU LIKE TO EAT?
HAMBURG SHTEAK? CURWY WICE?
Hmm...
PORRIDGE WOULD BE NICE...
Since I'm sick.
WENT HOME
GOTTA STOCK UP!!
WHAT'S POR-WIDGE?
IT'S WHEN YOU BOIL RICE SO IT'S SOFT.
RICE PUDDING.
OH! SO CLOSE!
Did I get it wrong?
It's amazing.
OH, BUT...
IT'S COOL AND SWEET, AND VERY EASY TO EAT.
THE MILD MILKY FLAVOR WAS VERY GOOD.

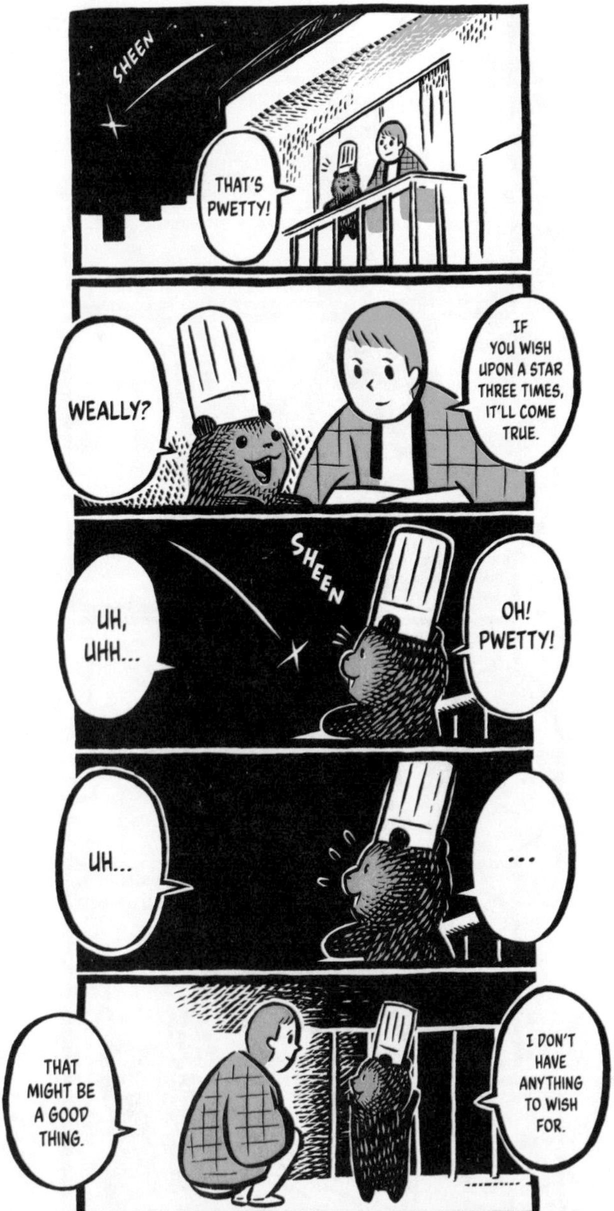
SHEEN
THAT'S PWETTY!
IF YOU WISH UPON A STAR THREE TIMES, IT'LL COME TRUE.
WEALLY?
OH! PWETTY!
SHEEN
UH, UHH...
...
UH...
I DON'T HAVE ANYTHING TO WISH FOR.
THAT MIGHT BE A GOOD THING.

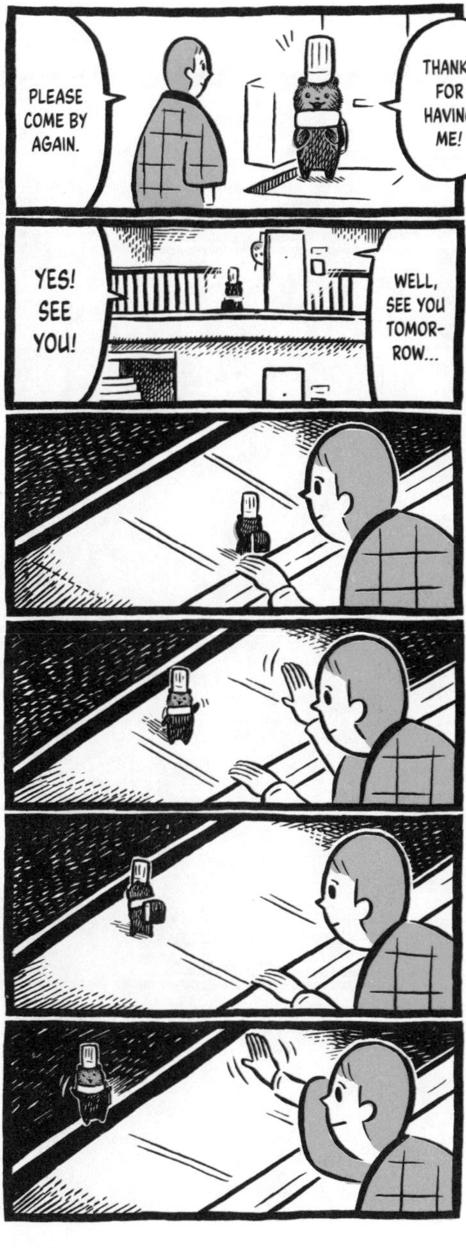
THANKS FOR HAVING ME!
PLEASE COME BY AGAIN.
WELL, SEE YOU TOMOR-ROW...
YES! SEE YOU!

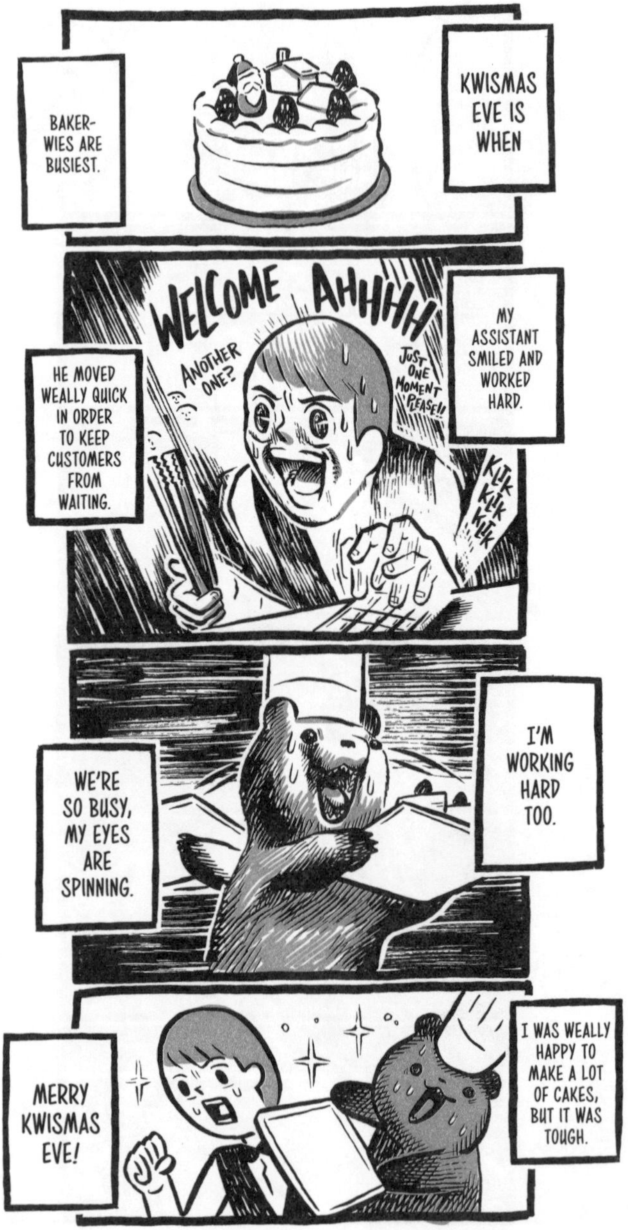
KWISMAS EVE IS WHEN
BAKER-WIES ARE BUSIEST.
MY ASSISTANT SMILED AND WORKED HARD.
AHHHH
WELCOME
JUST ONE MOMENT PLEASE!!
ANOTHER ONE?
HE MOVED WEALLY QUICK IN ORDER TO KEEP CUSTOMERS FROM WAITING.
KLIK KLIK KLIK
I'M WORKING HARD TOO.
WE'RE SO BUSY, MY EYES ARE SPINNING.
I WAS WEALLY HAPPY TO MAKE A LOT OF CAKES, BUT IT WAS TOUGH.
MERRY KWISMAS EVE!

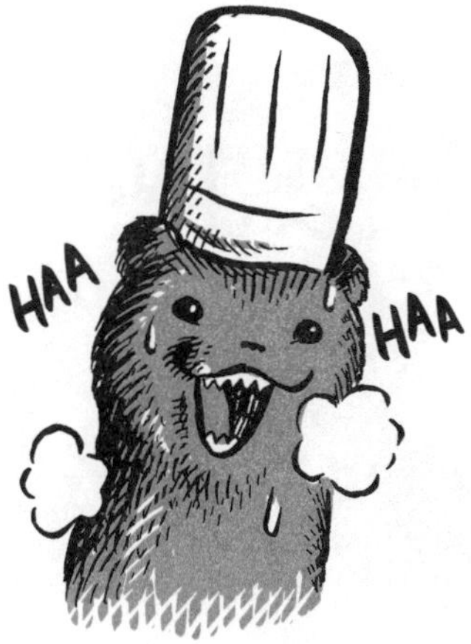
HAA
HAA

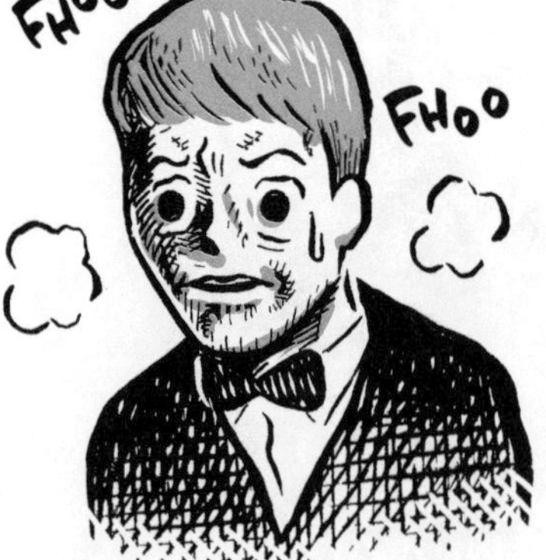
FHOO
FHOO

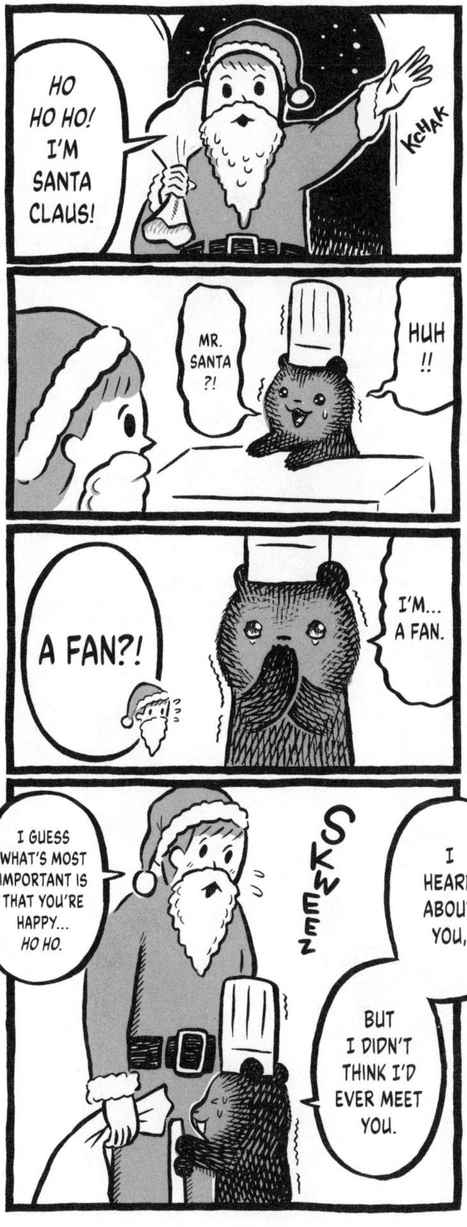
KCHAK
HO HO HO! I'M SANTA CLAUS!
HUH!!
MR. SANTA?!
I'M... A FAN.
A FAN?!
I HEARD ABOUT YOU,
BUT I DIDN'T THINK I'D EVER MEET YOU.
SKWEEZ
I GUESS WHAT'S MOST IMPORTANT IS THAT YOU'RE HAPPY... HO HO.

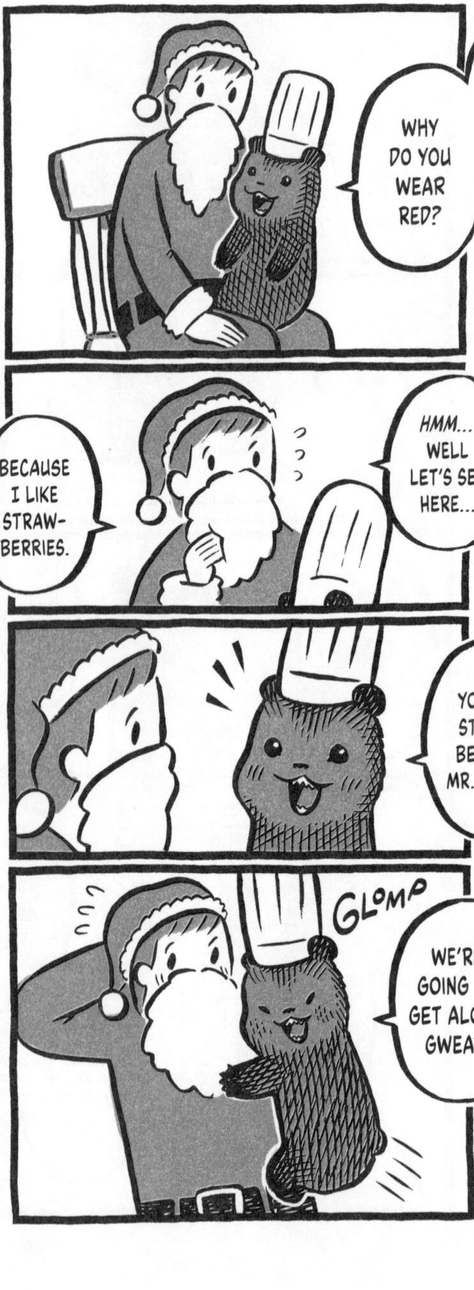
MR. SANTA,
WHY DO YOU WEAR RED?
HMM... WELL LET'S SEE HERE...
BECAUSE I LIKE STRAW-BERRIES.
YOU LIKE STWAW-BERWIES, MR. SANTA?
GLOMP
WE'RE GOING TO GET ALONG GWEAT!

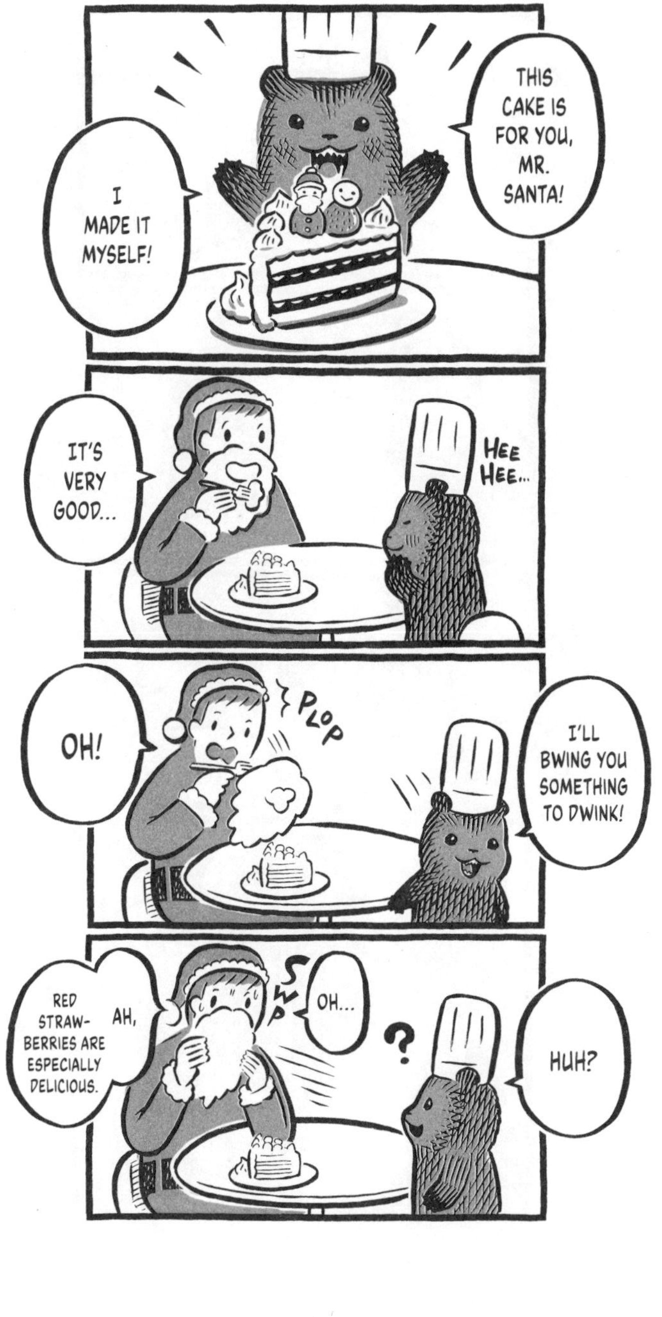
THIS CAKE IS FOR YOU, MR. SANTA!
I MADE IT MYSELF!
HEE HEE...
IT'S VERY GOOD...
I'LL BWING YOU SOMETHING TO DWINK!
PLOP
OH!
HUH?
OH...
SWP
AH, RED STRAW-BERRIES ARE ESPECIALLY DELICIOUS.

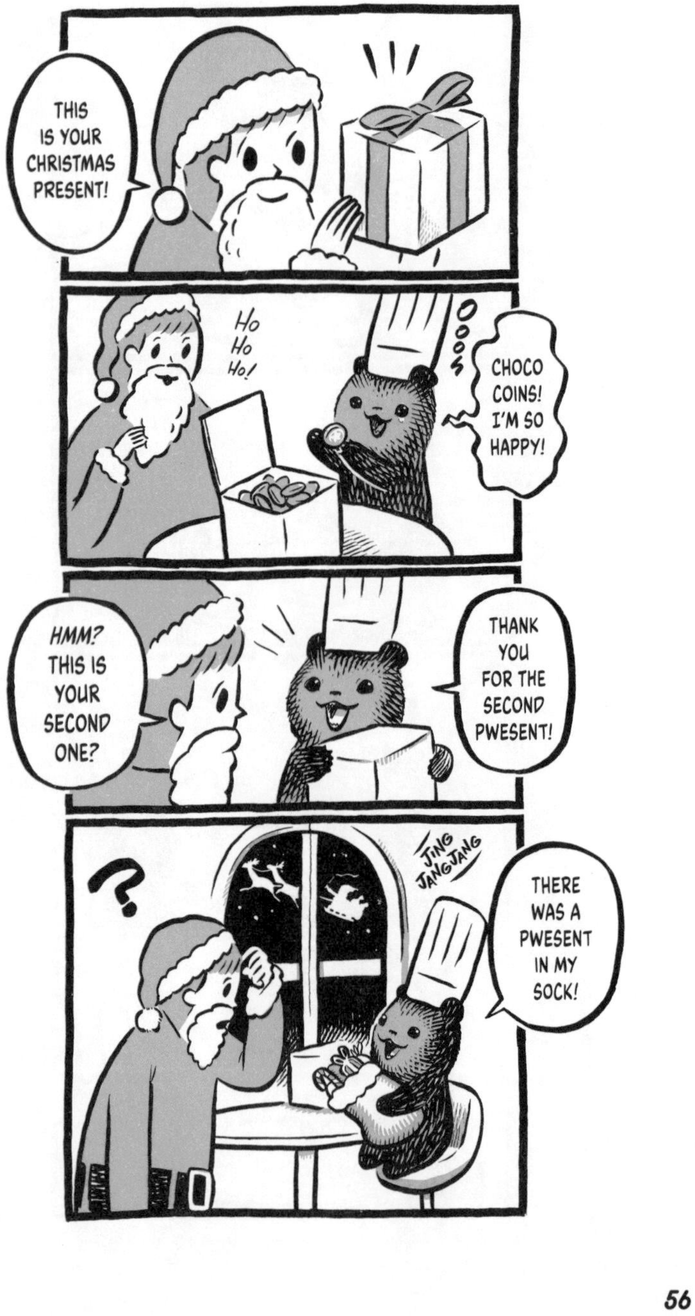
THIS IS YOUR CHRISTMAS PRESENT!
CHOCO COINS! I'M SO HAPPY!
Ooo
Ho Ho Ho!
THANK YOU FOR THE SECOND PWESENT!
HMM? THIS IS YOUR SECOND ONE?
THERE WAS A PWESENT IN MY SOCK!
JING JANGJANG
?

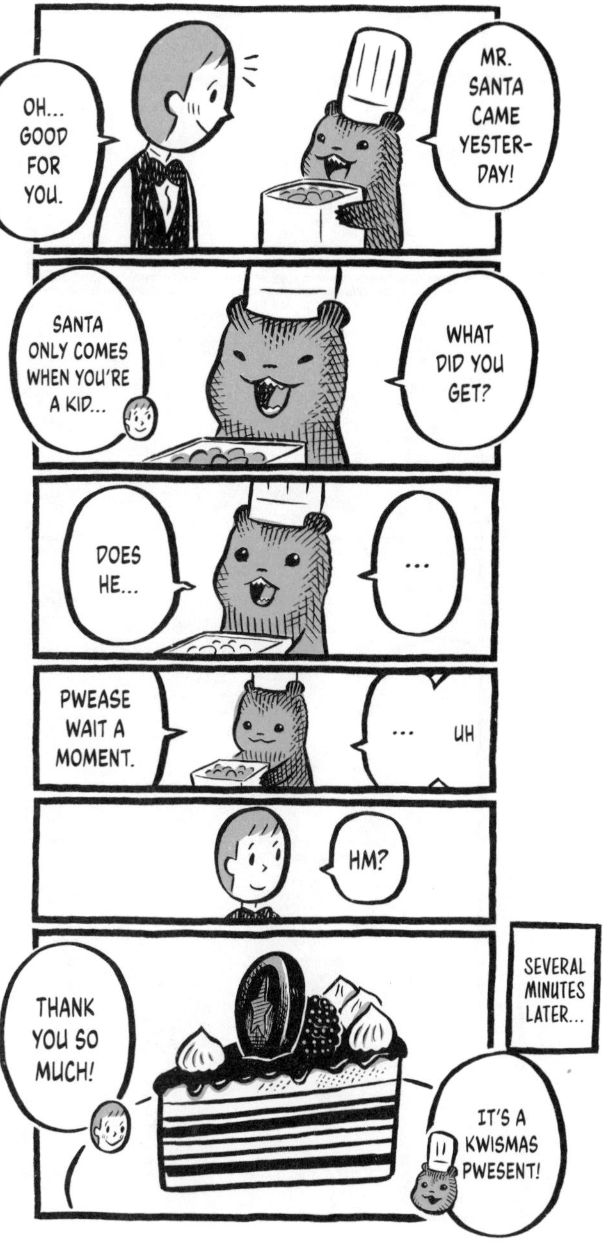
MR. SANTA CAME YESTER-DAY!
OH... GOOD FOR YOU.
WHAT DID YOU GET?
SANTA ONLY COMES WHEN YOU'RE A KID...
...
DOES HE...
... UH
PWEASE WAIT A MOMENT.
HM?
SEVERAL MINUTES LATER...
IT'S A KWISMAS PWESENT!
THANK YOU SO MUCH!

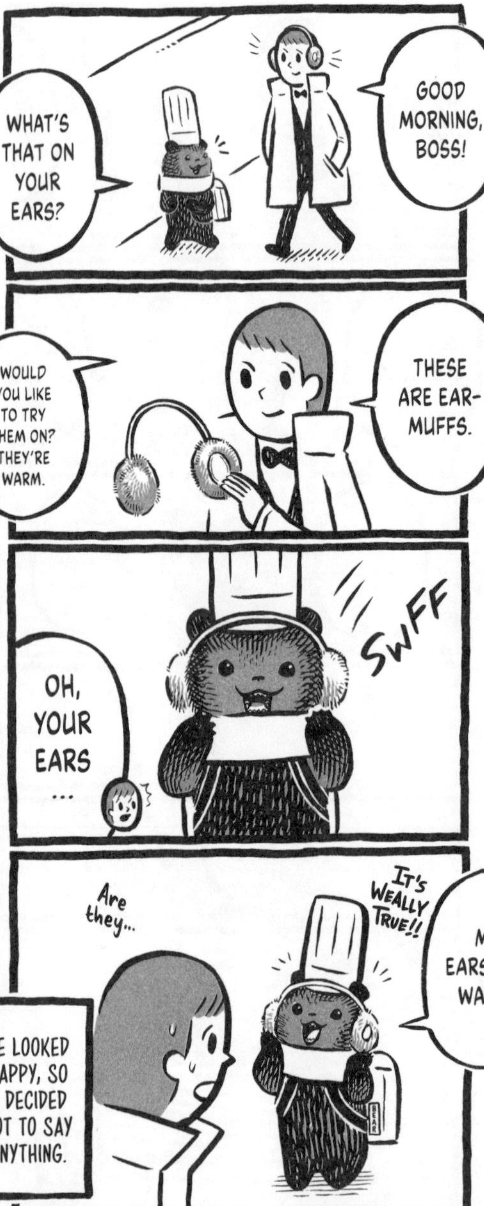
GOOD MORNING, BOSS!
WHAT'S THAT ON YOUR EARS?
THESE ARE EAR-MUFFS.
WOULD YOU LIKE TO TRY THEM ON? THEY'RE WARM.
SWFF
OH, YOUR EARS ...
MY EARS ARE WARM!
IT'S WEALLY TRUE!!
Are they...
BEAR
HE LOOKED HAPPY, SO I DECIDED NOT TO SAY ANYTHING.

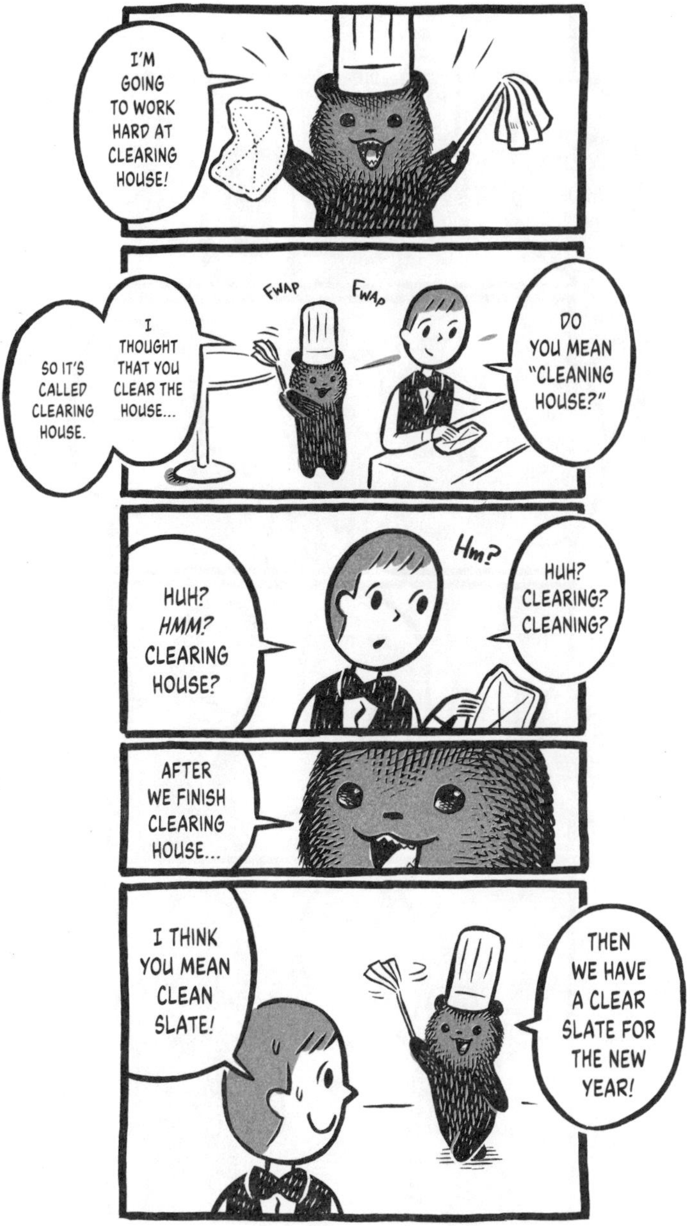
I'M GOING TO WORK HARD AT CLEARING HOUSE!
DO YOU MEAN "CLEANING HOUSE?"
FWAP
FWAP
I THOUGHT THAT YOU CLEAR THE HOUSE...
SO IT'S CALLED CLEARING HOUSE.
Hm?
HUH? CLEARING? CLEANING?
HUH? *HMM?* CLEARING HOUSE?
AFTER WE FINISH CLEARING HOUSE...
THEN WE HAVE A CLEAR SLATE FOR THE NEW YEAR!
I THINK YOU MEAN CLEAN SLATE!

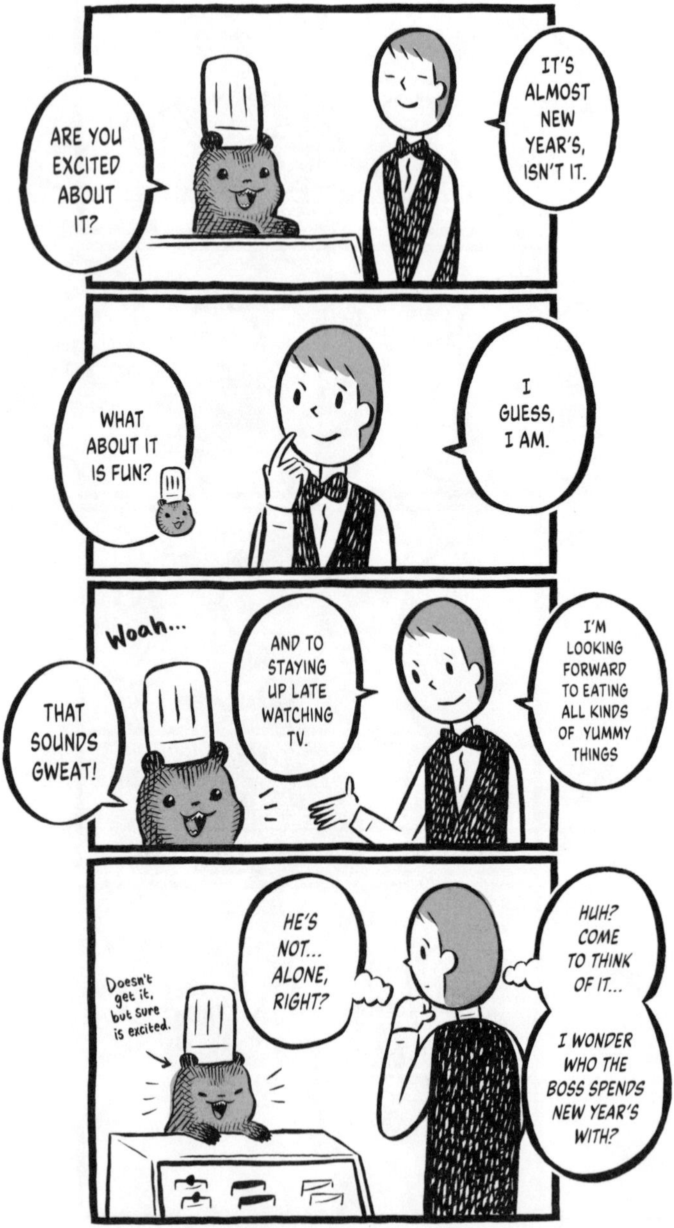
IT'S ALMOST NEW YEAR'S, ISN'T IT.
ARE YOU EXCITED ABOUT IT?
I GUESS, I AM.
WHAT ABOUT IT IS FUN?
I'M LOOKING FORWARD TO EATING ALL KINDS OF YUMMY THINGS
AND TO STAYING UP LATE WATCHING TV.
Woah...
THAT SOUNDS GWEAT!
HUH? COME TO THINK OF IT...
I WONDER WHO THE BOSS SPENDS NEW YEAR'S WITH?
HE'S NOT... ALONE, RIGHT?
Doesn't get it, but sure is excited.

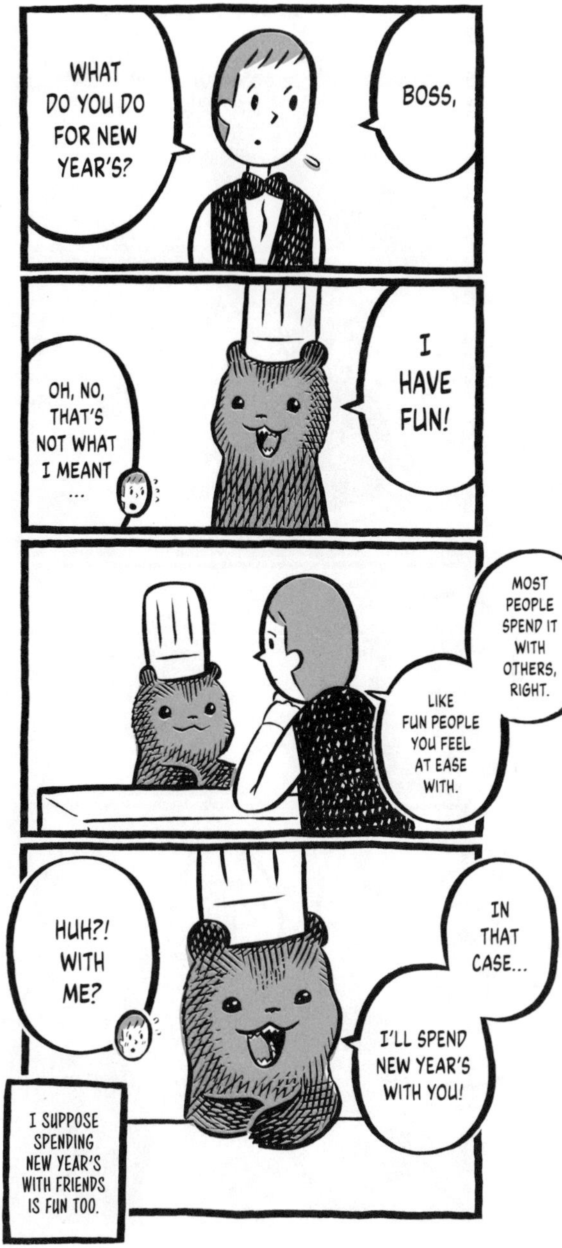
BOSS,
WHAT DO YOU DO FOR NEW YEAR'S?
I HAVE FUN!
OH, NO, THAT'S NOT WHAT I MEANT ...
MOST PEOPLE SPEND IT WITH OTHERS, RIGHT.
LIKE FUN PEOPLE YOU FEEL AT EASE WITH.
IN THAT CASE...
I'LL SPEND NEW YEAR'S WITH YOU!
HUH?! WITH ME?
I SUPPOSE SPENDING NEW YEAR'S WITH FRIENDS IS FUN TOO.

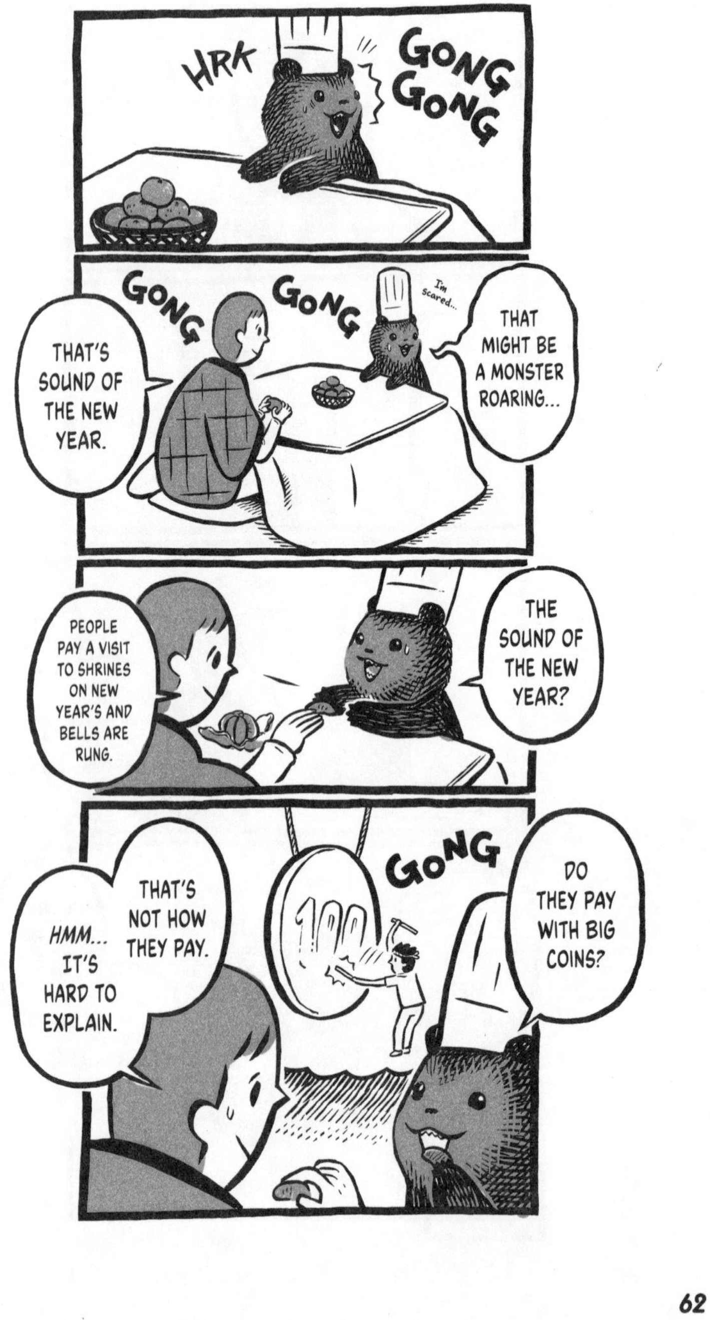
GONG
GONG
HRK
I'm scared...
THAT MIGHT BE A MONSTER ROARING...
GONG
GONG
THAT'S SOUND OF THE NEW YEAR.
THE SOUND OF THE NEW YEAR?
PEOPLE PAY A VISIT TO SHRINES ON NEW YEAR'S AND BELLS ARE RUNG.
DO THEY PAY WITH BIG COINS?
GONG
100
THAT'S NOT HOW THEY PAY.
HMM... IT'S HARD TO EXPLAIN.

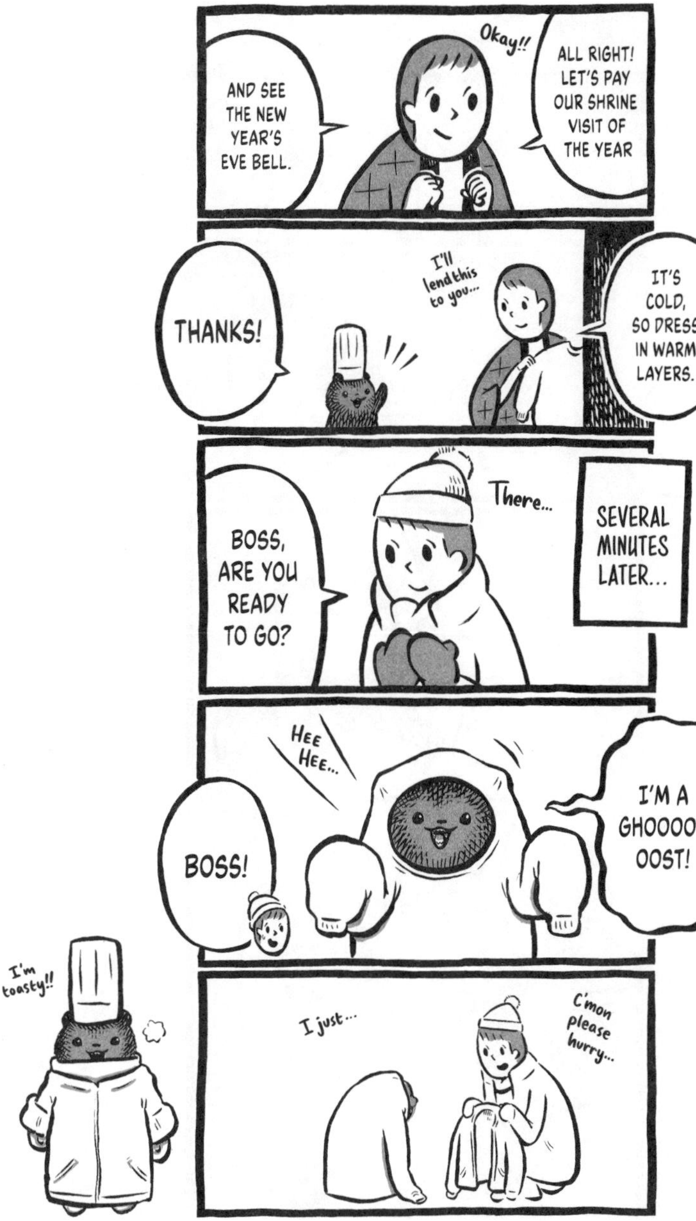
ALL RIGHT! LET'S PAY OUR SHRINE VISIT OF THE YEAR
Okay!!
AND SEE THE NEW YEAR'S EVE BELL.
IT'S COLD, SO DRESS IN WARM LAYERS.
I'll lend this to you...
THANKS!
SEVERAL MINUTES LATER...
There...
BOSS, ARE YOU READY TO GO?
I'M A GHOOOO-OOST!
HEE HEE...
BOSS!
C'mon please hurry...
I just...
I'm toasty!!

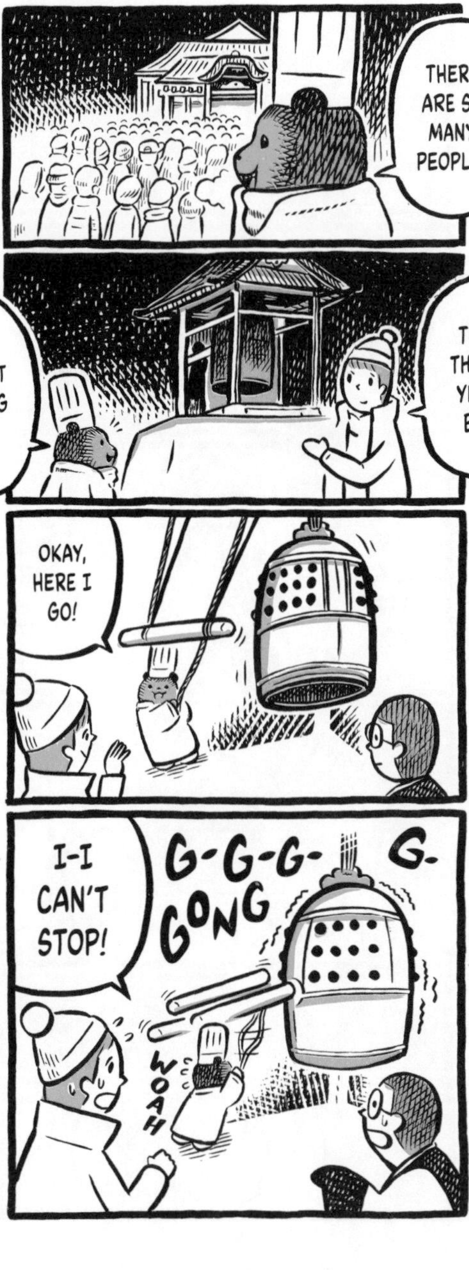
THERE ARE SO MANY PEOPLE!
THAT'S THE NEW YEAR'S BELL.
I WANT TO RING IT!
OKAY, HERE I GO!
G-
G-G-G-
GONG
I-I CAN'T STOP!
WOAH

I'M GOING TO FLY THE KITE,
SO PLEASE KEEP A TIGHT HOLD OF IT, BOSS.
TMP
FWOO

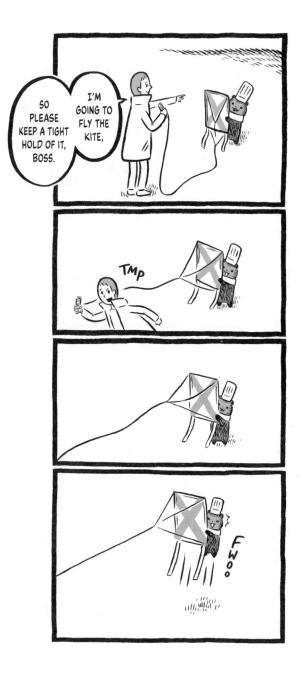

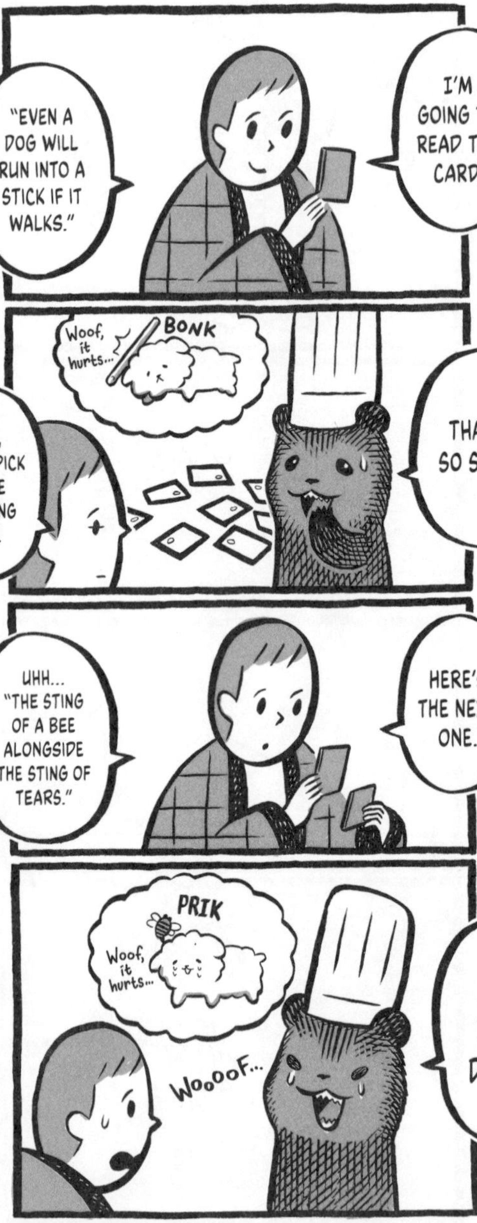
I'M GOING TO READ THE CARD.
"EVEN A DOG WILL RUN INTO A STICK IF IT WALKS."
BONK
Woof, it hurts...
THAT'S SO SAD...
BOSS, PLEASE PICK UP THE MATCHING CARD.
HERE'S THE NEXT ONE.
UHH... "THE STING OF A BEE ALONGSIDE THE STING OF TEARS."
PRIK
Woof, it hurts...
THAT POOR DOGGY!
WoooOF...

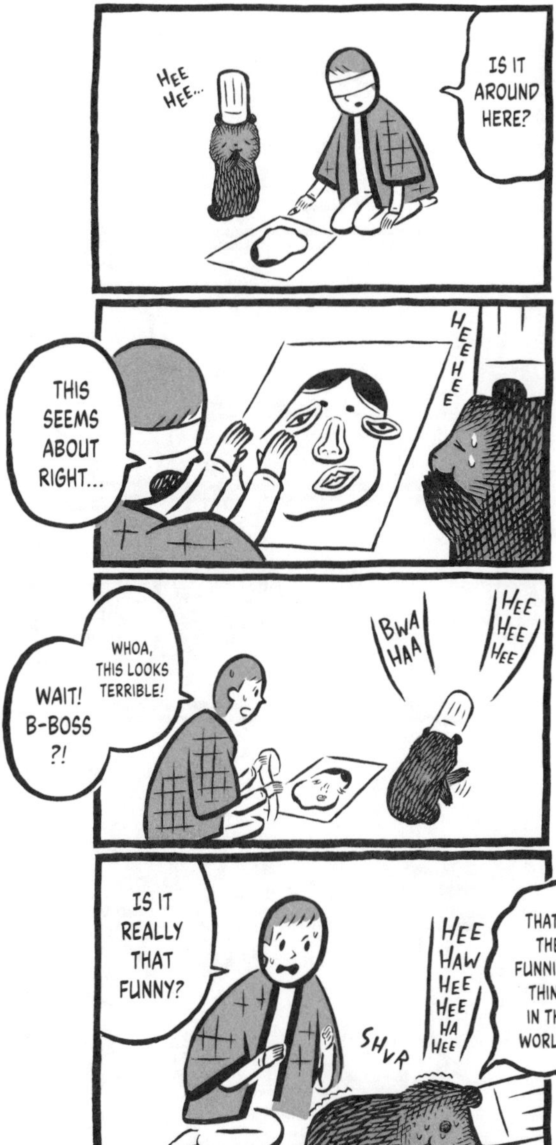
IS IT AROUND HERE?
HEE HEE...
HEE HEE
THIS SEEMS ABOUT RIGHT...
HEE HEE HEE
BWA HAA
WHOA, THIS LOOKS TERRIBLE!
WAIT! B-BOSS ?!
THAT'S THE FUNNIEST THING IN THE WORLD!!
HEE HAW HEE HEE HA HEE
IS IT REALLY THAT FUNNY?
SHVR

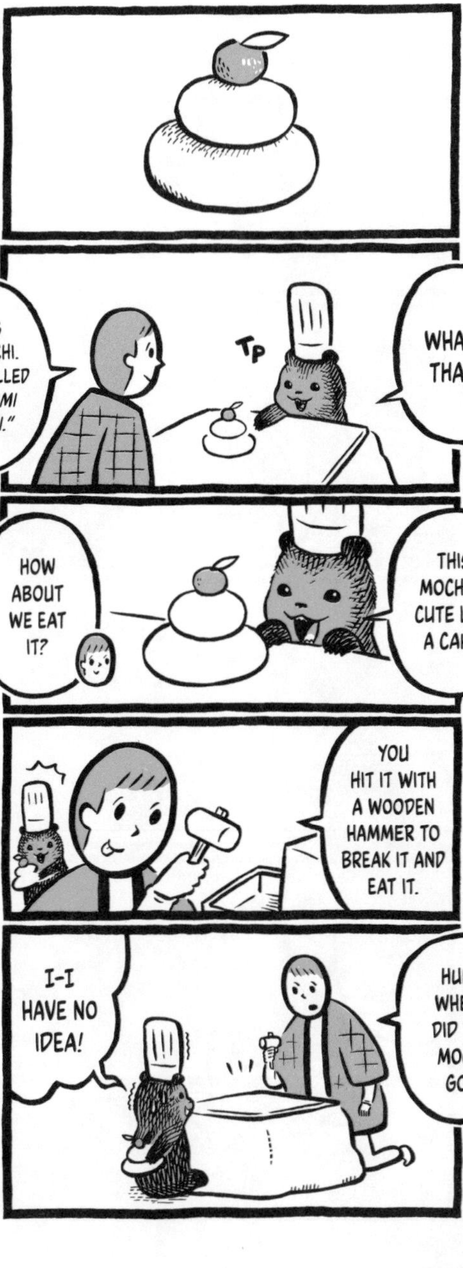
WHAT'S THAT?
TP
THIS IS MOCHI. IT'S CALLED "KAGAMI MOCHI."
THIS MOCHI IS CUTE LIKE A CAKE.
HOW ABOUT WE EAT IT?
YOU HIT IT WITH A WOODEN HAMMER TO BREAK IT AND EAT IT.
HUH? WHERE DID THE MOCHI GO?
I-I HAVE NO IDEA!
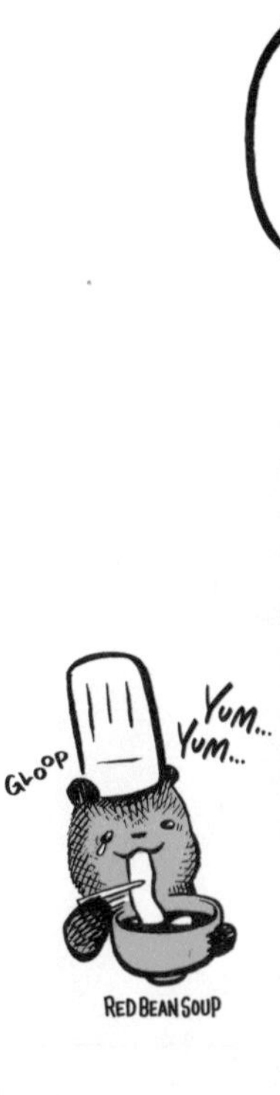
Yum... Yum...
GLOOP
RED BEAN SOUP

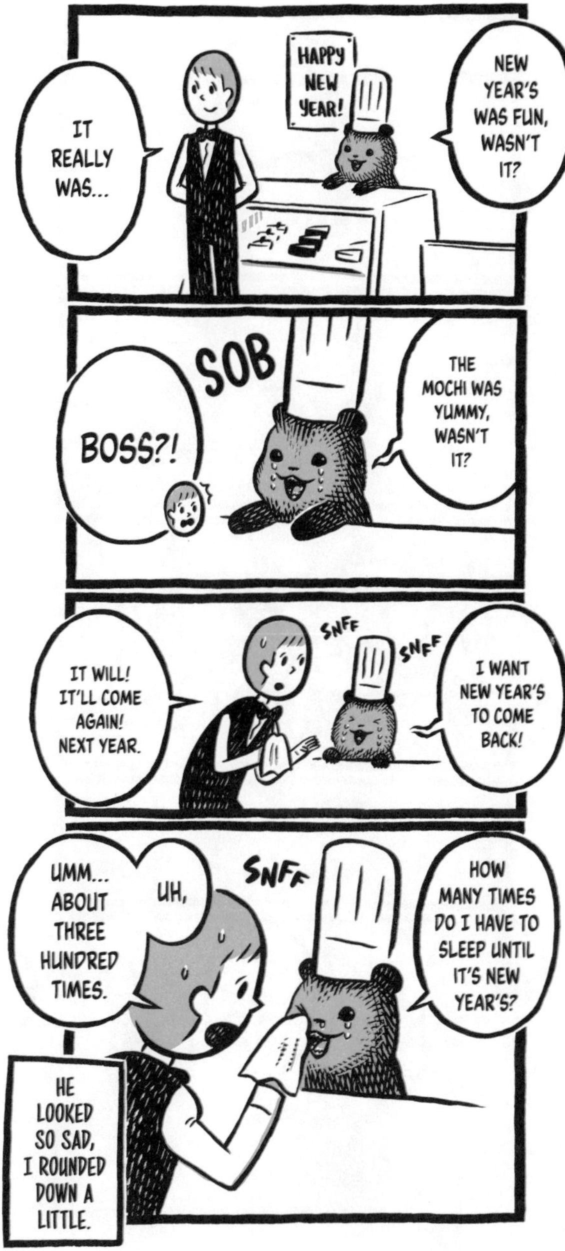
HAPPY NEW YEAR!
NEW YEAR'S WAS FUN, WASN'T IT?
IT REALLY WAS...
THE MOCHI WAS YUMMY, WASN'T IT?
SOB
BOSS?!
I WANT NEW YEAR'S TO COME BACK!
SNFF
SNFF
IT WILL! IT'LL COME AGAIN! NEXT YEAR.
HOW MANY TIMES DO I HAVE TO SLEEP UNTIL IT'S NEW YEAR'S?
SNFF
UH,
UMM... ABOUT THREE HUNDRED TIMES.
HE LOOKED SO SAD, I ROUNDED DOWN A LITTLE.

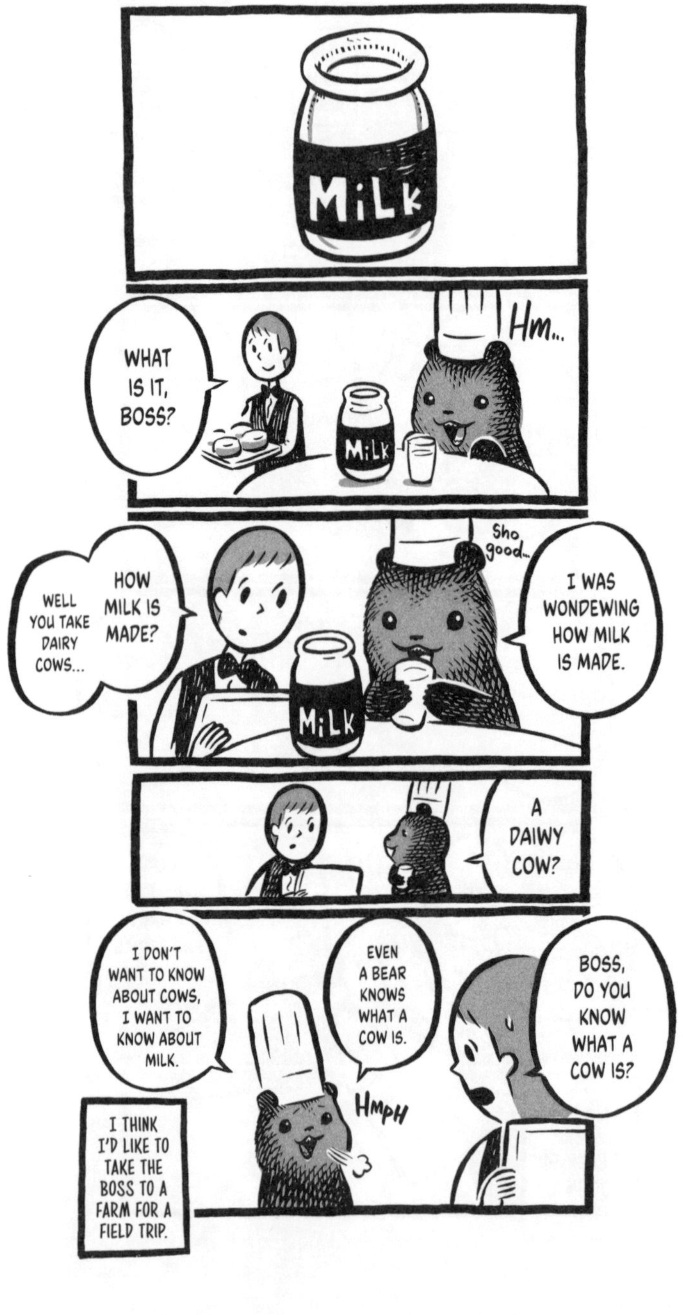
MiLk
Hm...
WHAT IS IT, BOSS?
MiLk
Sho good...
I WAS WONDEWING HOW MILK IS MADE.
HOW MILK IS MADE?
WELL YOU TAKE DAIRY COWS...
MiLk
A DAIWY COW?
BOSS, DO YOU KNOW WHAT A COW IS?
EVEN A BEAR KNOWS WHAT A COW IS.
I DON'T WANT TO KNOW ABOUT COWS, I WANT TO KNOW ABOUT MILK.
HMPH
I THINK I'D LIKE TO TAKE THE BOSS TO A FARM FOR A FIELD TRIP.

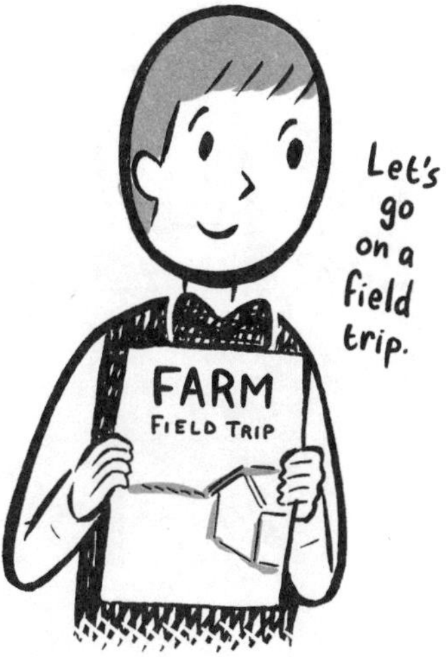
FARM
FIELD TRIP
Let's go on a field trip.

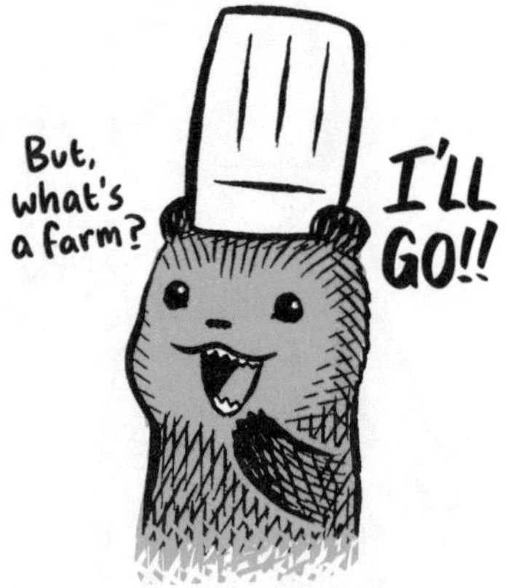
But, what's a farm?
I'LL GO!!

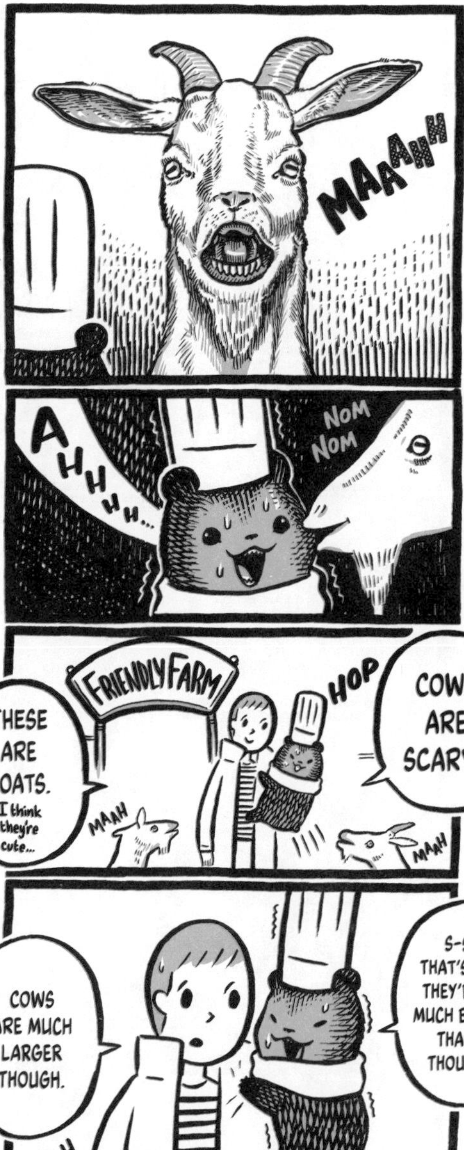
MAAAHH
NOM NOM
AHHHH...
COWS ARE SCARY!!
HOP
FRIENDLY FARM
THESE ARE GOATS.
I think they're cute...
MAAH
MAAH
S-SO THAT'S WHY THEY'RE SO MUCH BIGGER THAN I THOUGHT.
COWS ARE MUCH LARGER THOUGH.
MAAH

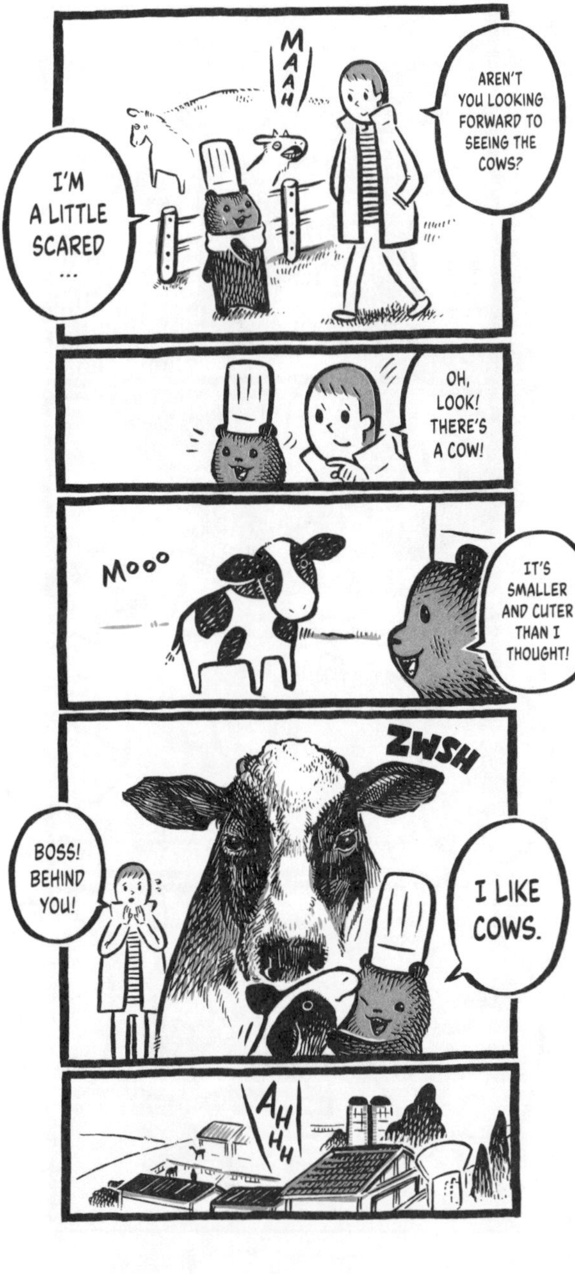
AREN'T YOU LOOKING FORWARD TO SEEING THE COWS?
MAAH
I'M A LITTLE SCARED ...
OH, LOOK! THERE'S A COW!
IT'S SMALLER AND CUTER THAN I THOUGHT!
Mooo
ZWSH
I LIKE COWS.
BOSS! BEHIND YOU!
AHHHH

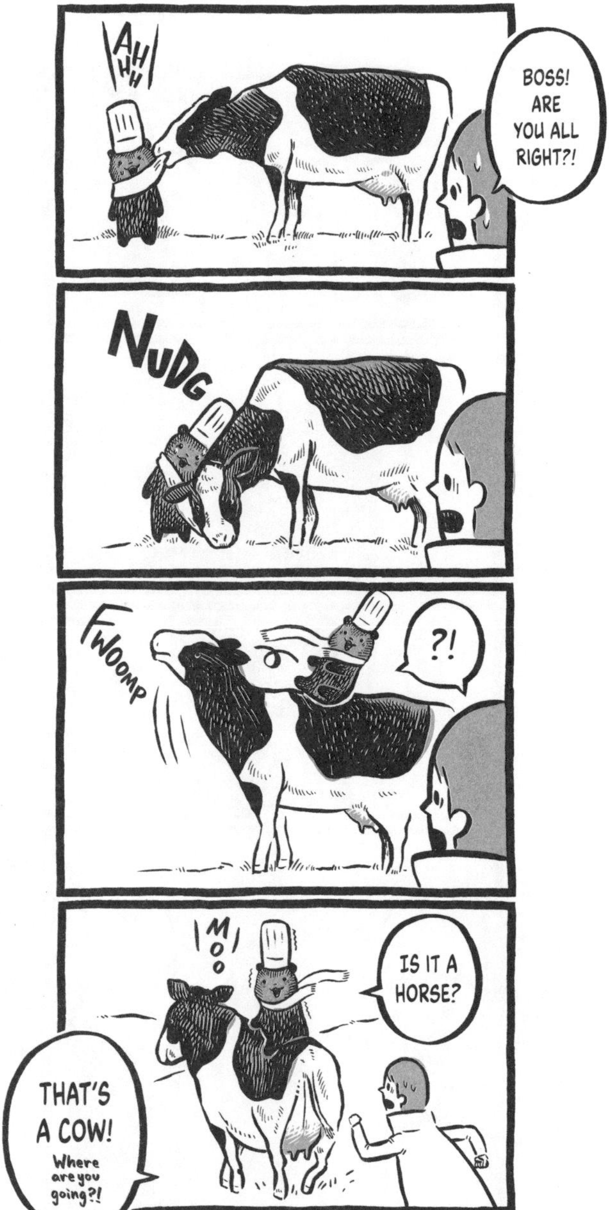
BOSS! ARE YOU ALL RIGHT?!
AHHH
NUDG
?!
FWOOMP
IS IT A HORSE?
MOO
THAT'S A COW!
Where are you going?!

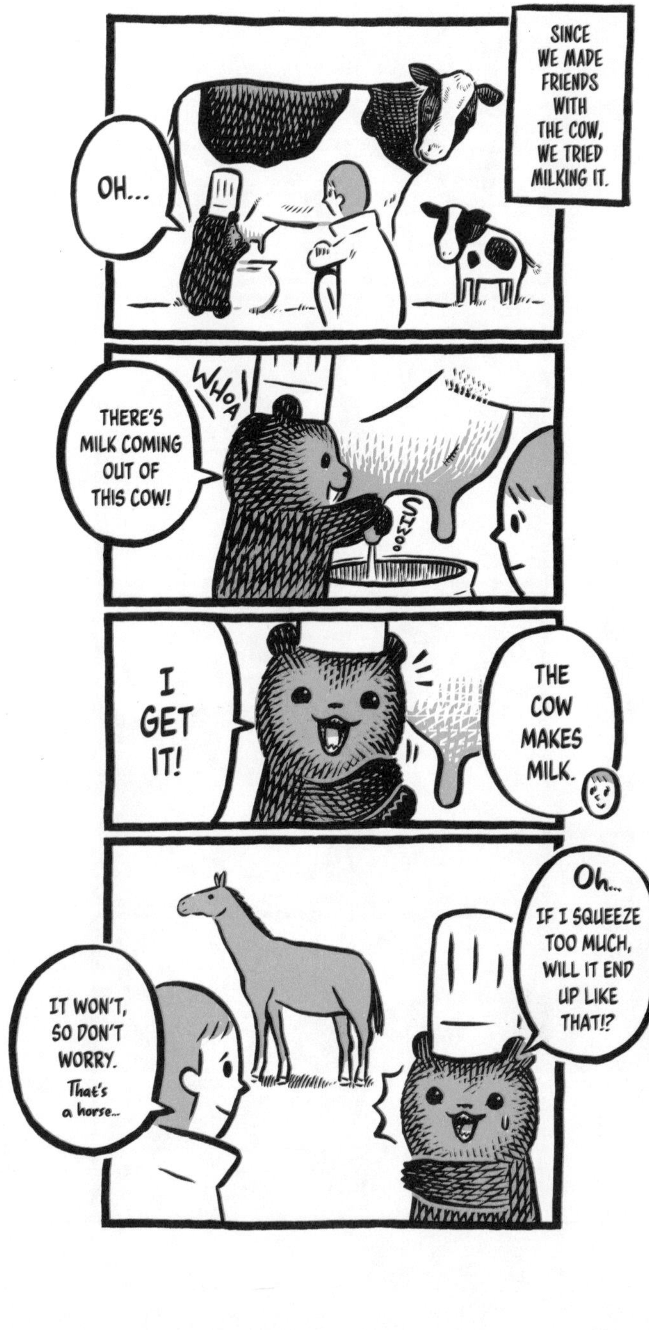
SINCE WE MADE FRIENDS WITH THE COW, WE TRIED MILKING IT.
OH...
WHOA
THERE'S MILK COMING OUT OF THIS COW!
SHWOO
THE COW MAKES MILK.
I GET IT!
Oh...
IF I SQUEEZE TOO MUCH, WILL IT END UP LIKE THAT!?
IT WON'T, SO DON'T WORRY.
That's a horse...

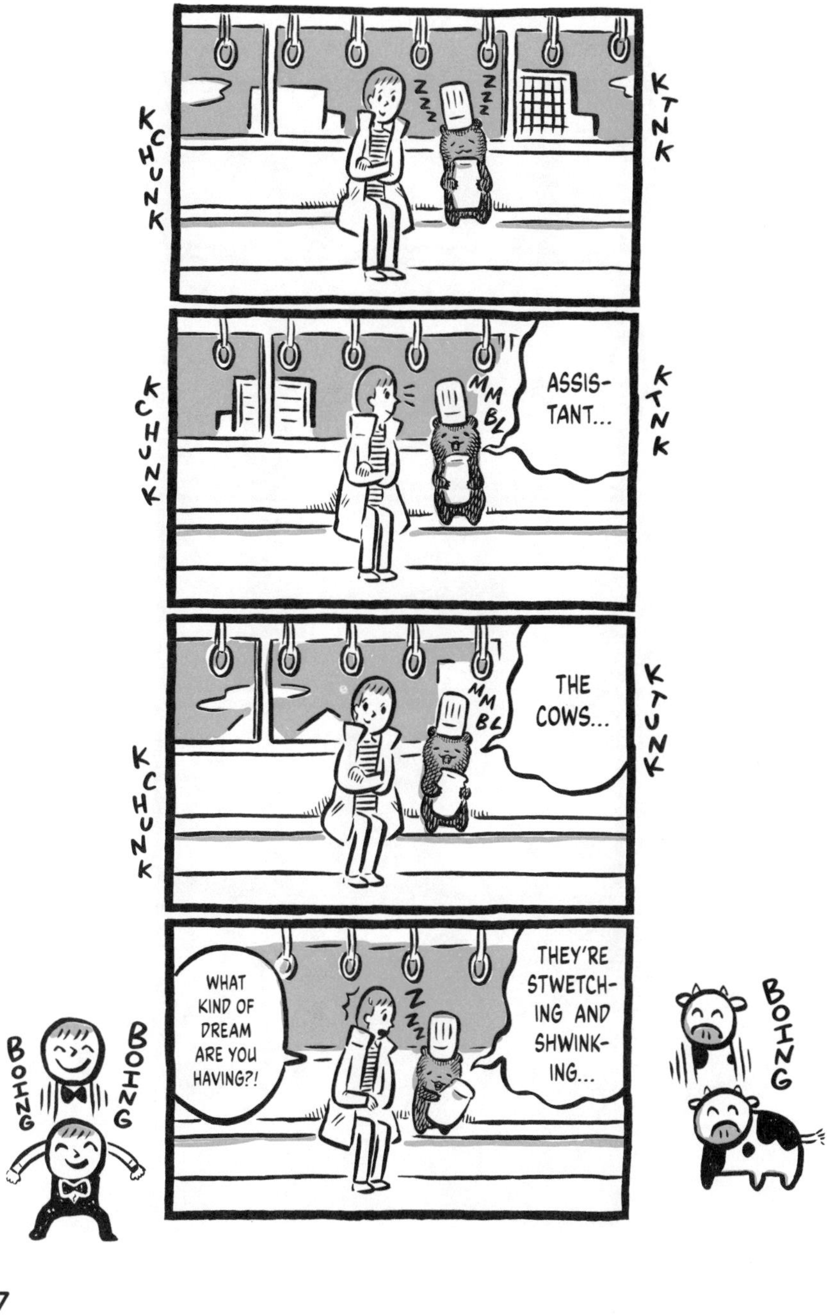
KTNK
ZZZ
ZZZ
KCHUNK
KTNK
ASSIS-TANT...
MMBL
KCHUNK
KTUNK
THE COWS...
MMBL
KCHUNK
BOING
THEY'RE STWETCH-ING AND SHWINK-ING...
ZZZ
WHAT KIND OF DREAM ARE YOU HAVING?!
BOING
BOING

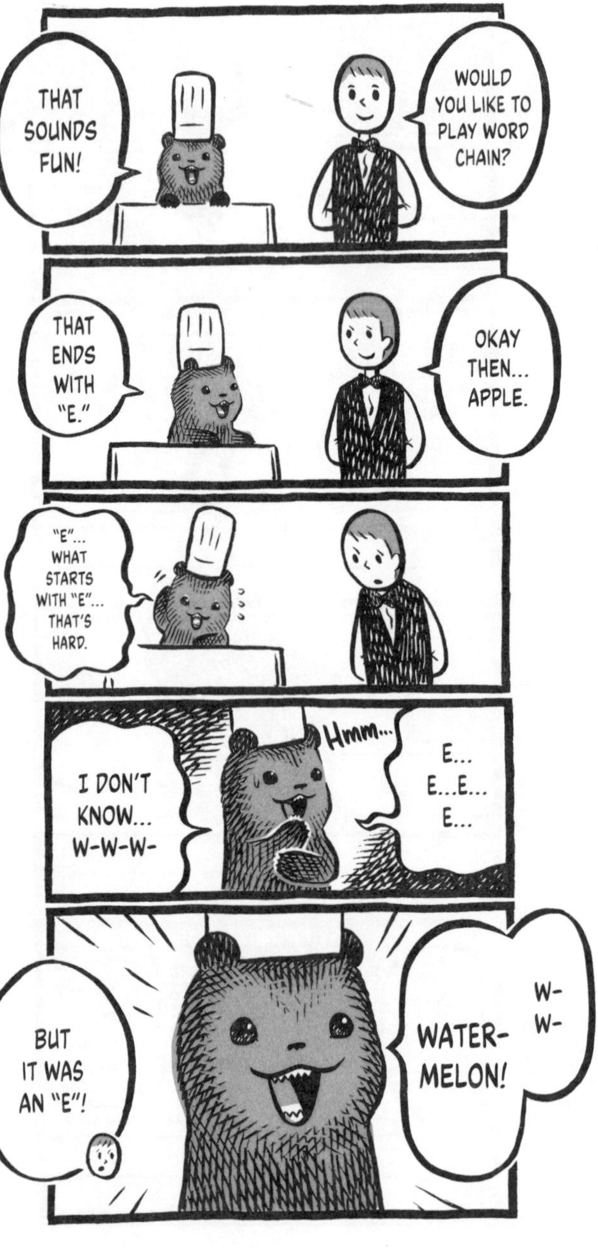
WOULD YOU LIKE TO PLAY WORD CHAIN?
THAT SOUNDS FUN!
OKAY THEN... APPLE.
THAT ENDS WITH "E."
"E"... WHAT STARTS WITH "E"... THAT'S HARD.
E... E...E... E...
Hmm...
I DON'T KNOW... W-W-W-
W- W-
WATER-MELON!
BUT IT WAS AN "E"!

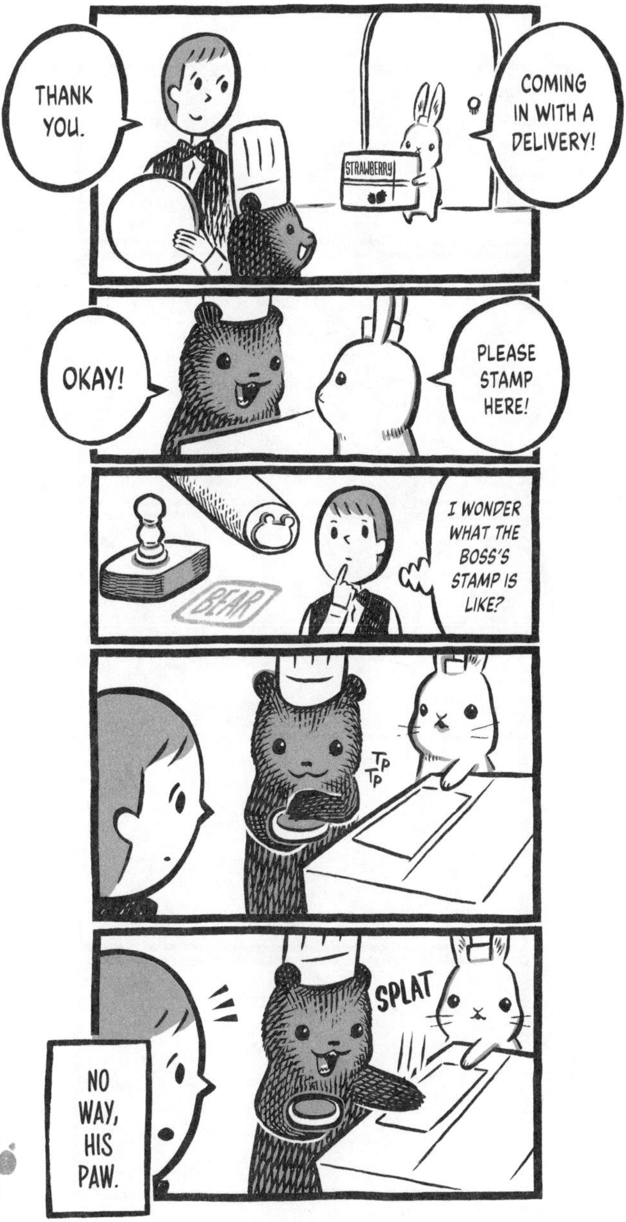
COMING IN WITH A DELIVERY!
STRAWBERRY
THANK YOU.
PLEASE STAMP HERE!
OKAY!
I WONDER WHAT THE BOSS'S STAMP IS LIKE?
BEAR
TP TP
SPLAT
NO WAY, HIS PAW.

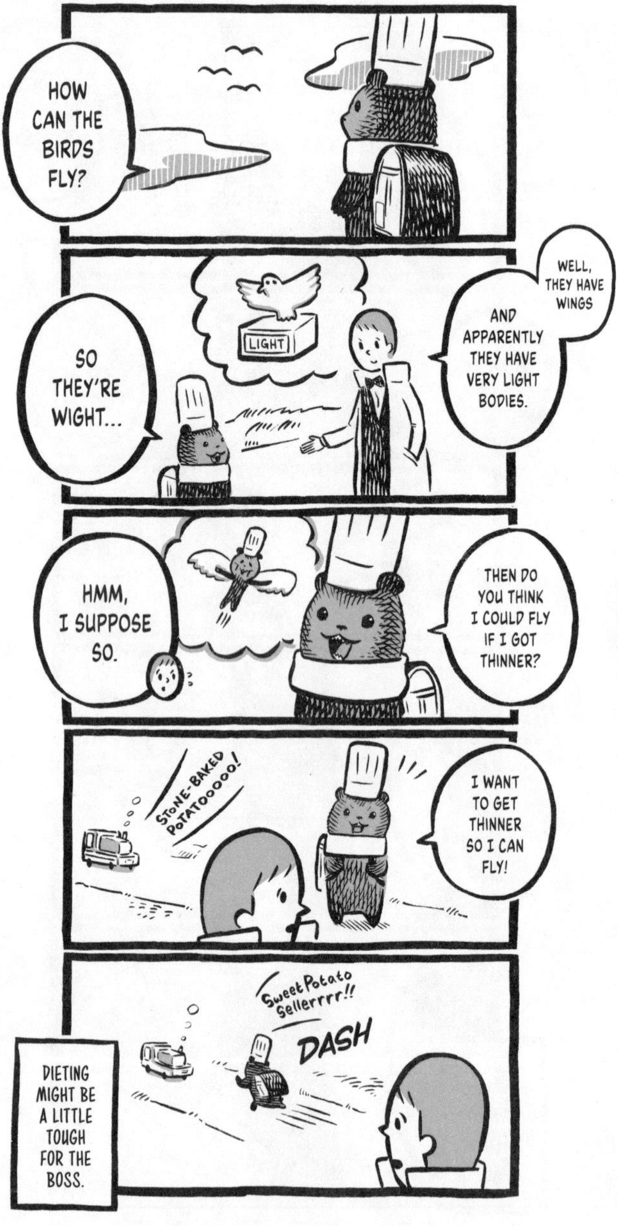
HOW CAN THE BIRDS FLY?
WELL, THEY HAVE WINGS
AND APPARENTLY THEY HAVE VERY LIGHT BODIES.
LIGHT
SO THEY'RE WIGHT...
THEN DO YOU THINK I COULD FLY IF I GOT THINNER?
HMM, I SUPPOSE SO.
I WANT TO GET THINNER SO I CAN FLY!
STONE-BAKED POTATOOOOO!
Sweet Potato Sellerrrr!!
DASH
DIETING MIGHT BE A LITTLE TOUGH FOR THE BOSS.

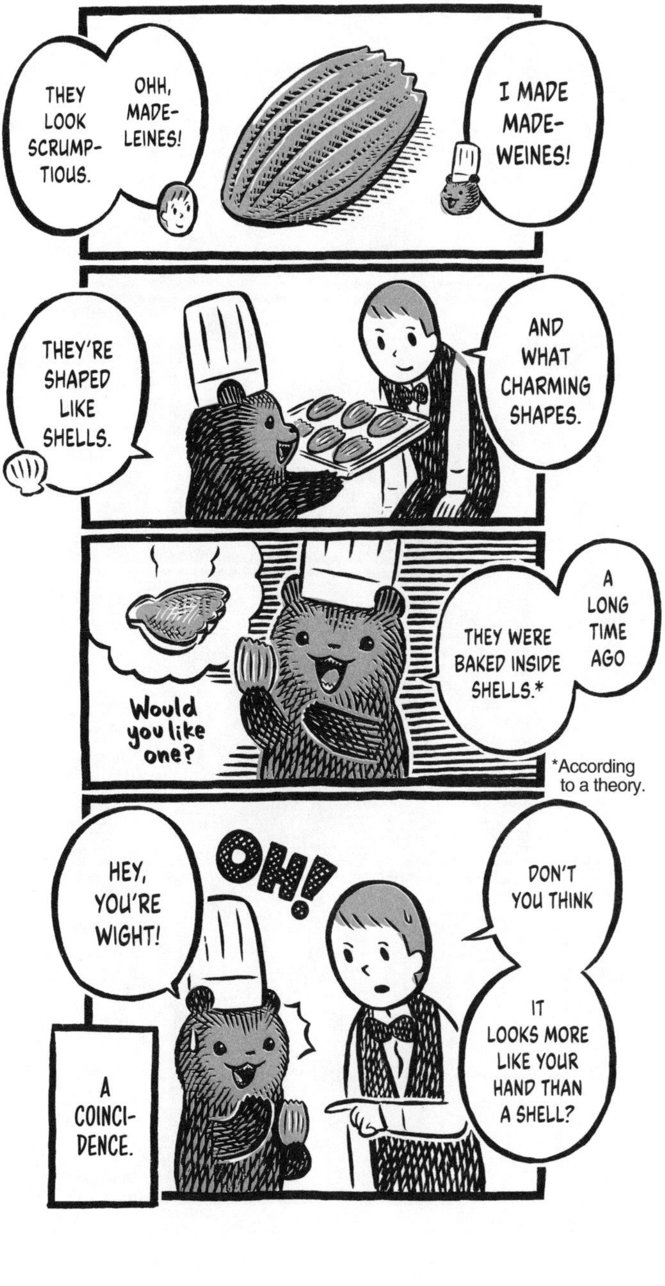
I MADE MADE-WEINES!
OHH, MADE-LEINES!
THEY LOOK SCRUMP-TIOUS.
AND WHAT CHARMING SHAPES.
THEY'RE SHAPED LIKE SHELLS.
A LONG TIME AGO
THEY WERE BAKED INSIDE SHELLS.*
Would you like one?
DON'T YOU THINK
IT LOOKS MORE LIKE YOUR HAND THAN A SHELL?
OH!
HEY, YOU'RE WIGHT!
A COINCI-DENCE.

*According to a theory.

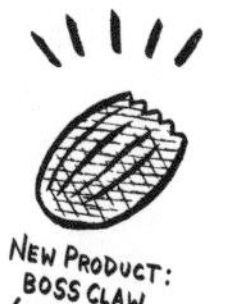
NEW PRODUCT: BOSS CLAW (Chocolate)

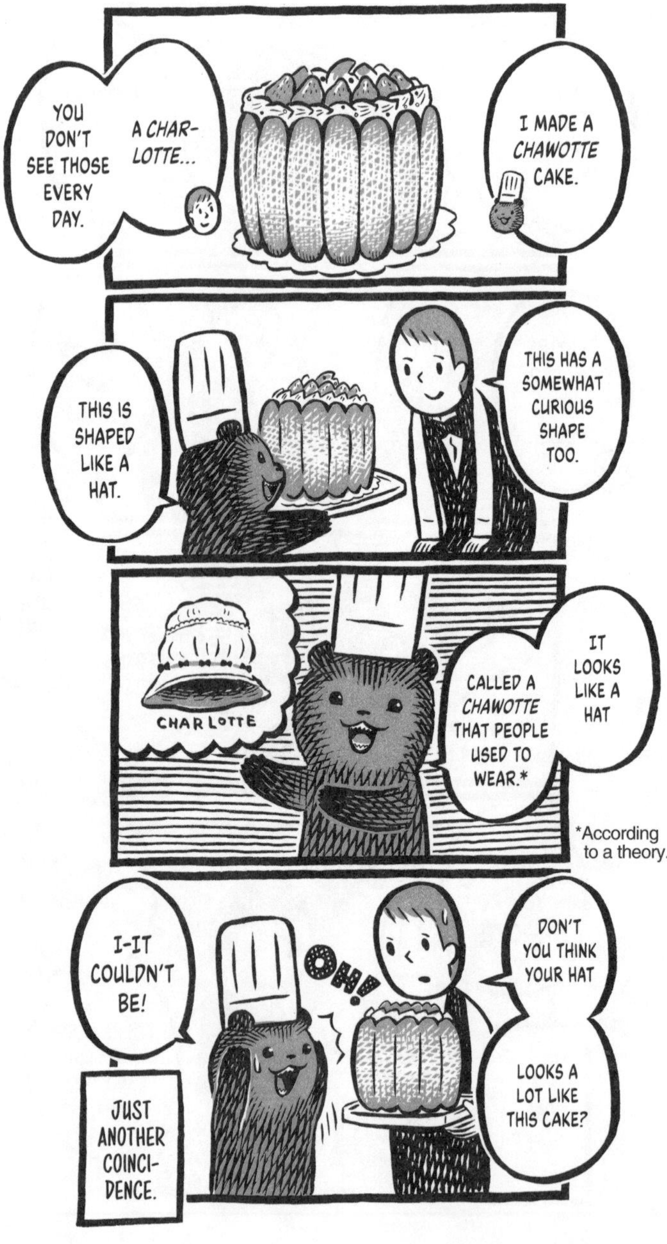
I MADE A *CHAWOTTE* CAKE.
A *CHAR-LOTTE*...
YOU DON'T SEE THOSE EVERY DAY.
THIS HAS A SOMEWHAT CURIOUS SHAPE TOO.
THIS IS SHAPED LIKE A HAT.
IT LOOKS LIKE A HAT
CALLED A *CHAWOTTE* THAT PEOPLE USED TO WEAR.*
CHARLOTTE
DON'T YOU THINK YOUR HAT
LOOKS A LOT LIKE THIS CAKE?
OH!
I-IT COULDN'T BE!
JUST ANOTHER COINCI-DENCE.

*According to a theory.

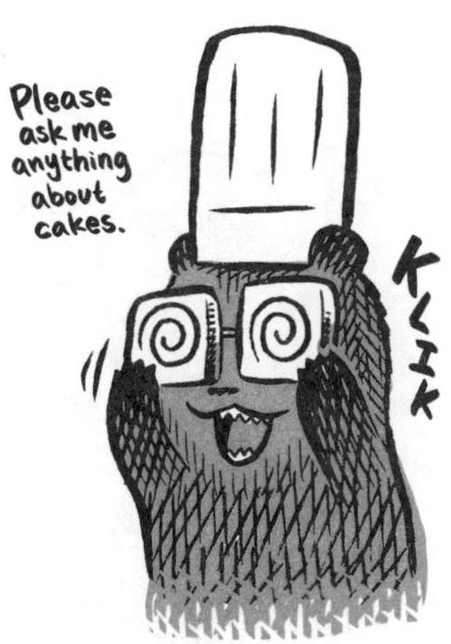
Please ask me anything about cakes.
KLIK

Where did those glasses come from?

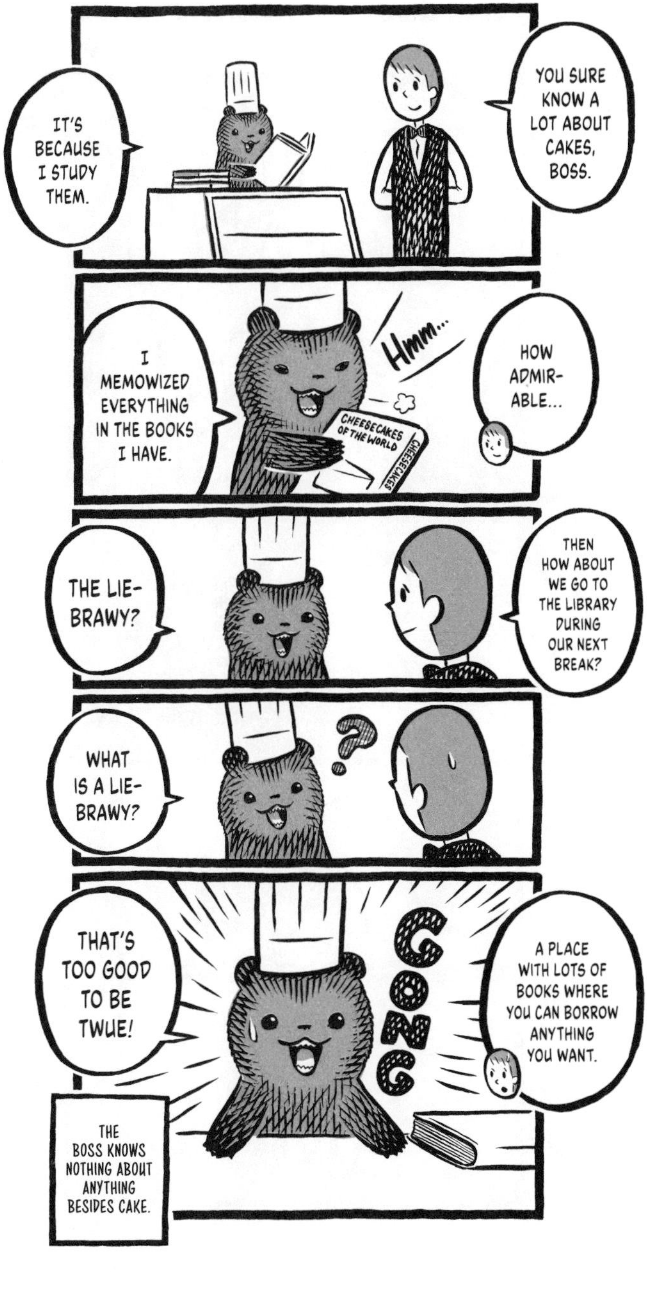
YOU SURE KNOW A LOT ABOUT CAKES, BOSS.
IT'S BECAUSE I STUDY THEM.
HOW ADMIR-ABLE...
Hmm...
CHEESECAKES OF THE WORLD
CHEESECAKES
I MEMOWIZED EVERYTHING IN THE BOOKS I HAVE.
THEN HOW ABOUT WE GO TO THE LIBRARY DURING OUR NEXT BREAK?
THE LIE-BRAWY?
WHAT IS A LIE-BRAWY?
A PLACE WITH LOTS OF BOOKS WHERE YOU CAN BORROW ANYTHING YOU WANT.
GONG
THAT'S TOO GOOD TO BE TWUE!
THE BOSS KNOWS NOTHING ABOUT ANYTHING BESIDES CAKE.

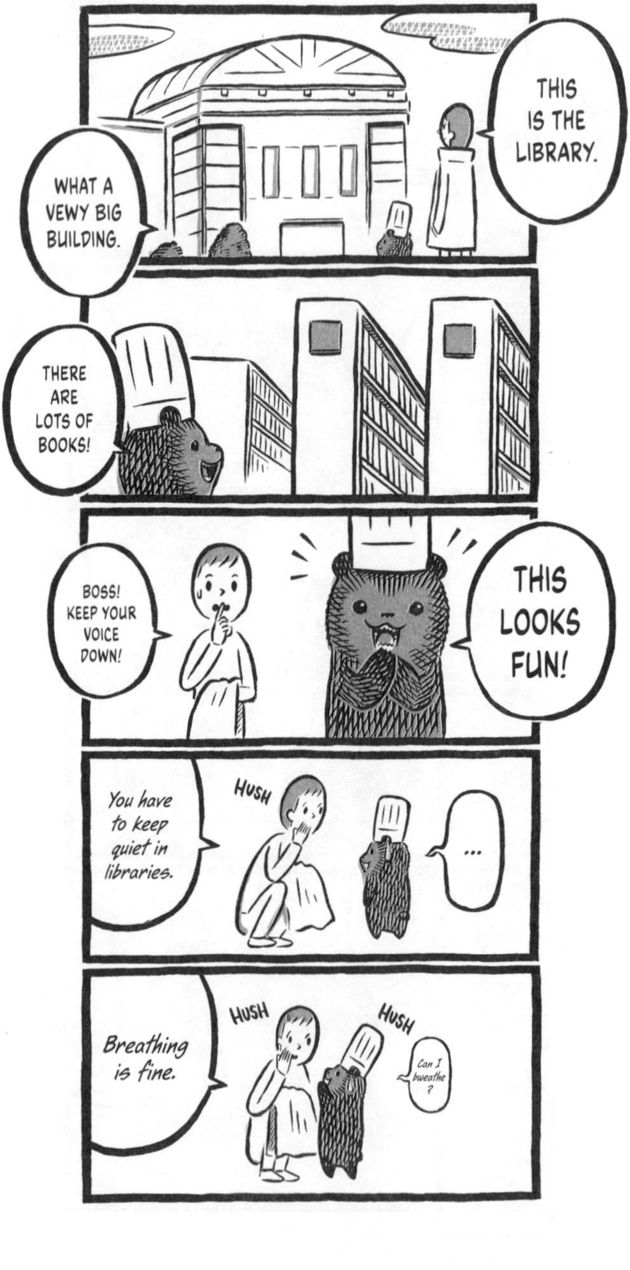

THIS IS THE LIBRARY.
WHAT A VEWY BIG BUILDING.
THERE ARE LOTS OF BOOKS!
THIS LOOKS FUN!
BOSS! KEEP YOUR VOICE DOWN!
...
HUSH
You have to keep quiet in libraries.
HUSH
Can I bweathe?
HUSH
Breathing is fine.

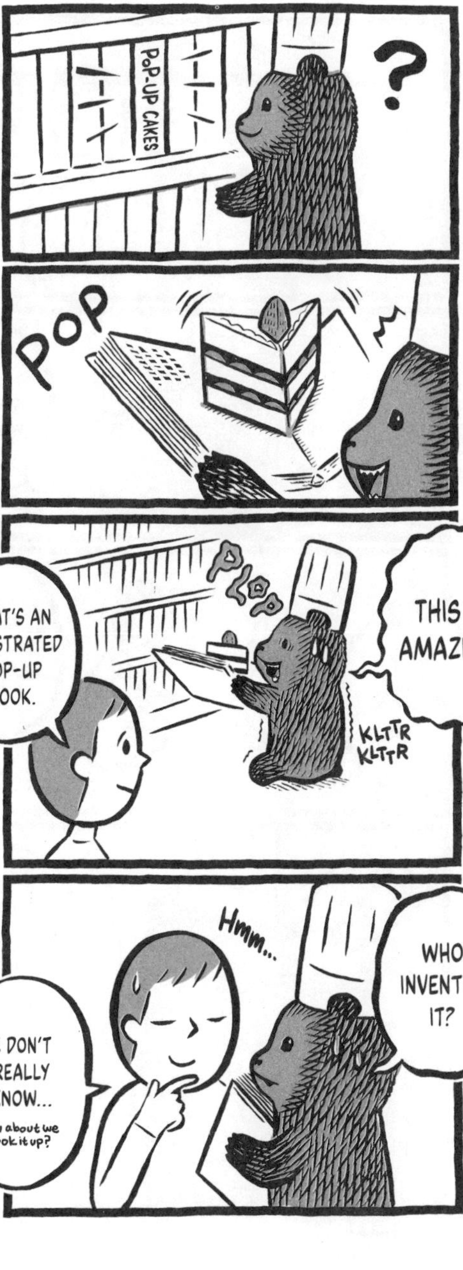
?
PoP-UP CAKES
POP
THIS IS AMAZING!
PLOP
THAT'S AN ILLUSTRATED POP-UP BOOK.
KLTTR KLTTR
WHO INVENTED IT?
Hmm...
I DON'T REALLY KNOW...
How about we look it up?

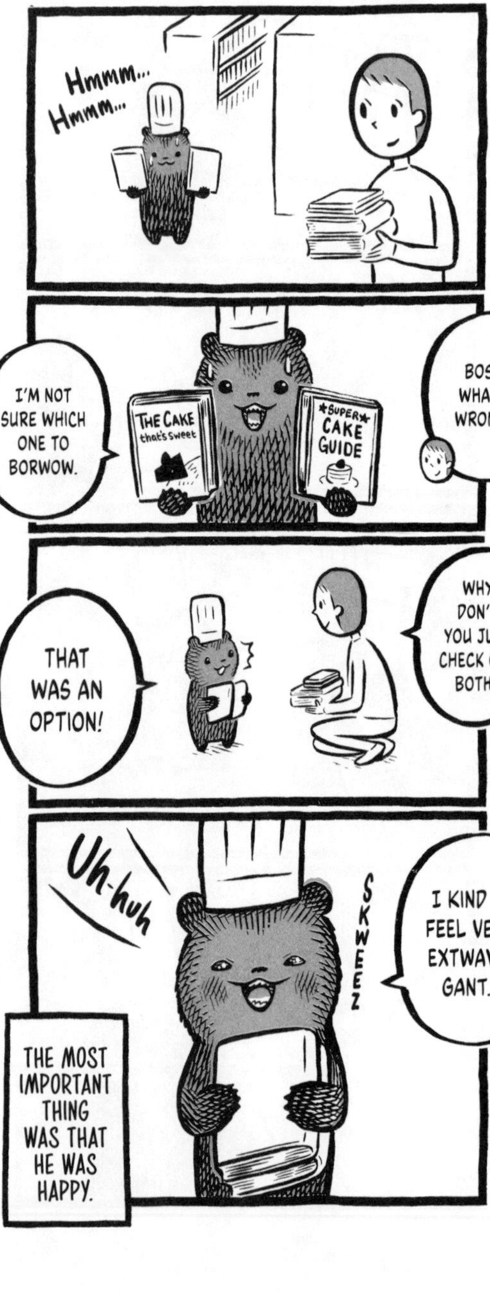
Hmmm... Hmmm...
BOSS, WHAT'S WRONG?
SUPER CAKE GUIDE
I'M NOT SURE WHICH ONE TO BORWOW.
THE CAKE that's sweet
WHY DON'T YOU JUST CHECK OUT BOTH?
THAT WAS AN OPTION!
I KIND OF FEEL VEWY EXTWAVA-GANT...
SKWEEZ
Uh-huh
THE MOST IMPORTANT THING WAS THAT HE WAS HAPPY.

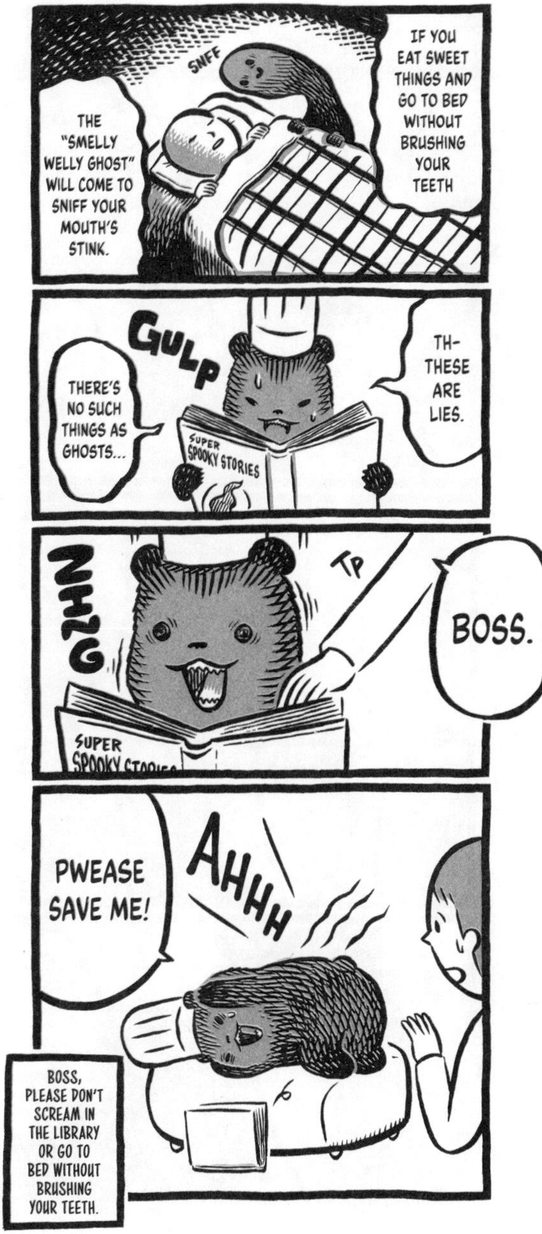
IF YOU EAT SWEET THINGS AND GO TO BED WITHOUT BRUSHING YOUR TEETH
SNFF
THE "SMELLY WELLY GHOST" WILL COME TO SNIFF YOUR MOUTH'S STINK.
TH- THESE ARE LIES.
GULP
SUPER SPOOKY STORIES
THERE'S NO SUCH THINGS AS GHOSTS...
BOSS.
TP
AHHH
PWEASE SAVE ME!
BOSS, PLEASE DON'T SCREAM IN THE LIBRARY OR GO TO BED WITHOUT BRUSHING YOUR TEETH.

WHAT ARE YOU READING?
A SCI-FI NOVEL.
WHAT IS IT ABOUT?
UM, SO...
TWO MEN GO TO THE MOON ON AN ADVENTURE
AND ARE CAPTURED BY ALIENS LIVING THERE.
UM, ASSIS-TANT...
WHAT IS IT?
I THINK THAT STOWY PROBABWY ISN'T REAL.
I KNOW THAT!

KNOWS HIS STUFF
There are lots of rabbits on the moon!!

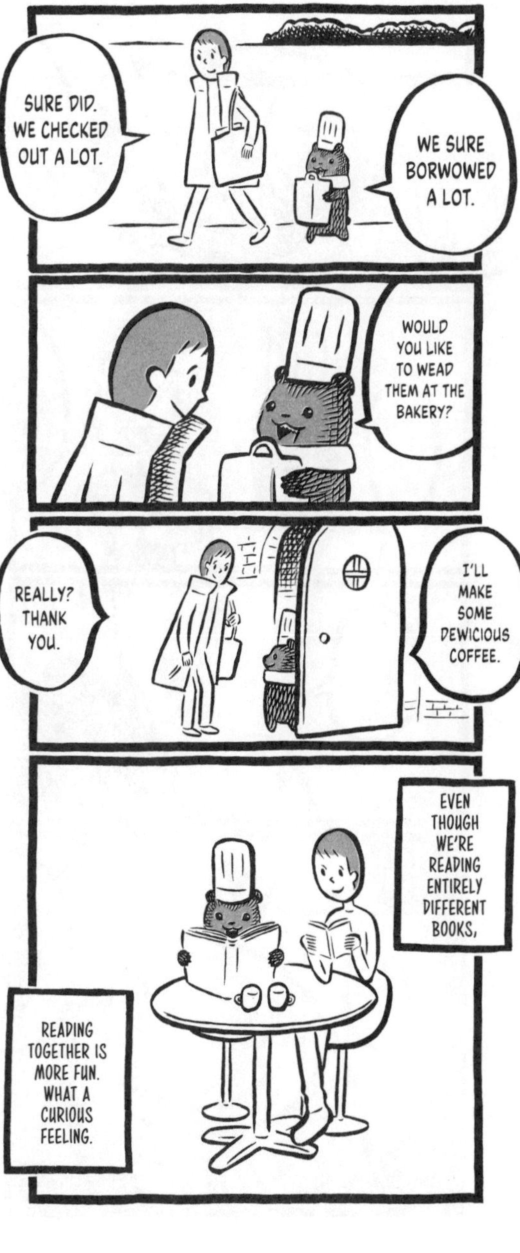
WE SURE BORWOWED A LOT.
SURE DID. WE CHECKED OUT A LOT.
WOULD YOU LIKE TO WEAD THEM AT THE BAKERY?
I'LL MAKE SOME DEWICIOUS COFFEE.
REALLY? THANK YOU.
EVEN THOUGH WE'RE READING ENTIRELY DIFFERENT BOOKS,
READING TOGETHER IS MORE FUN. WHAT A CURIOUS FEELING.

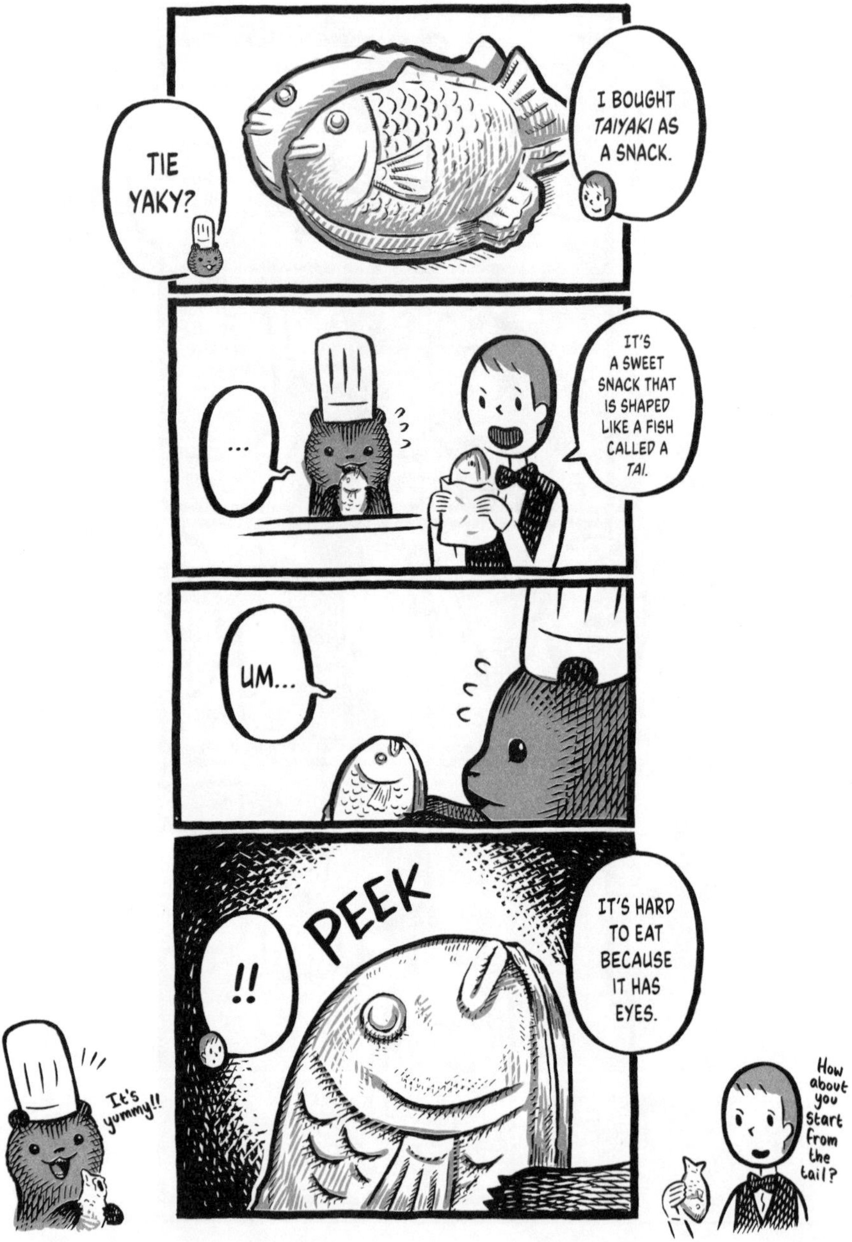
I BOUGHT *TAIYAKI* AS A SNACK.
TIE YAKY?
IT'S A SWEET SNACK THAT IS SHAPED LIKE A FISH CALLED A *TAI*.
...
UM...
IT'S HARD TO EAT BECAUSE IT HAS EYES.
PEEK
!!
How about you start from the tail?
It's yummy!!

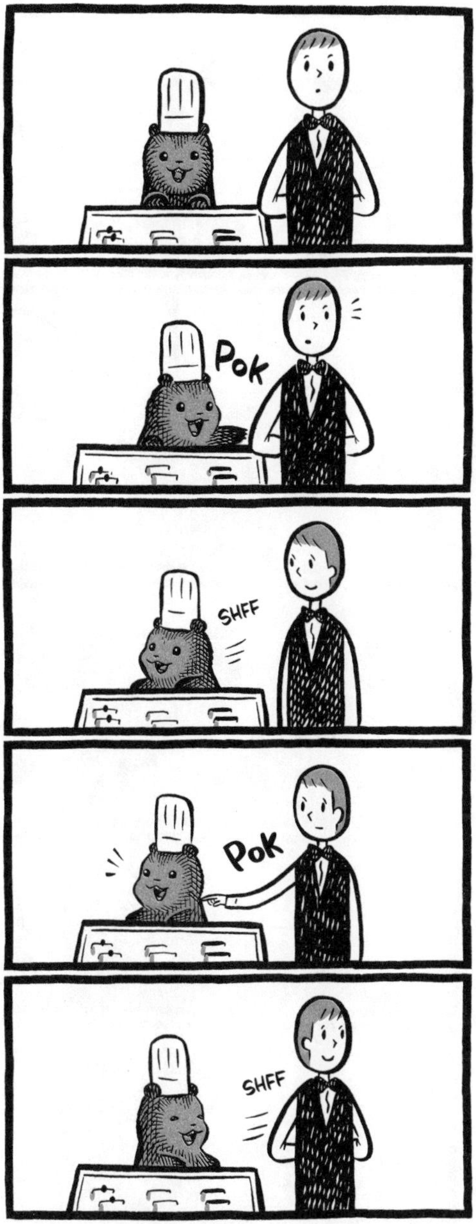
Pok
SHFF
Pok
SHFF

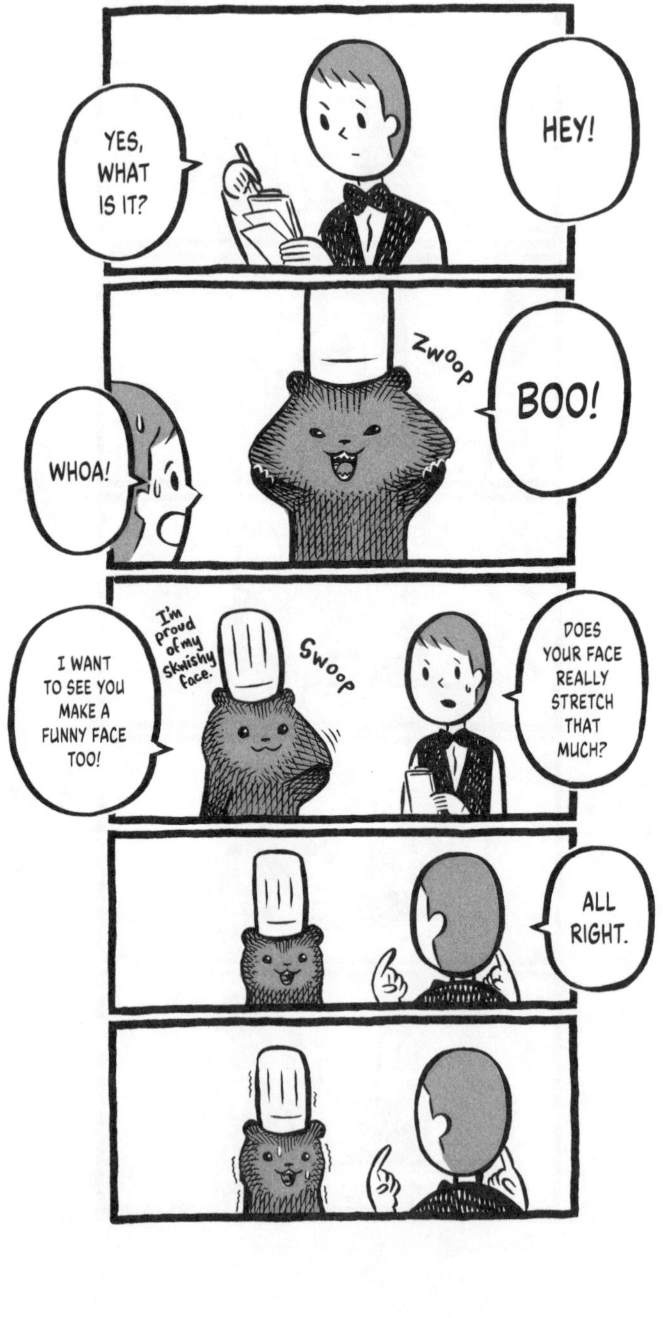
HEY!
YES, WHAT IS IT?
ZWOOP
BOO!
WHOA!
DOES YOUR FACE REALLY STRETCH THAT MUCH?
SWOOP
I'm proud of my skwishy face.
I WANT TO SEE YOU MAKE A FUNNY FACE TOO!
ALL RIGHT.

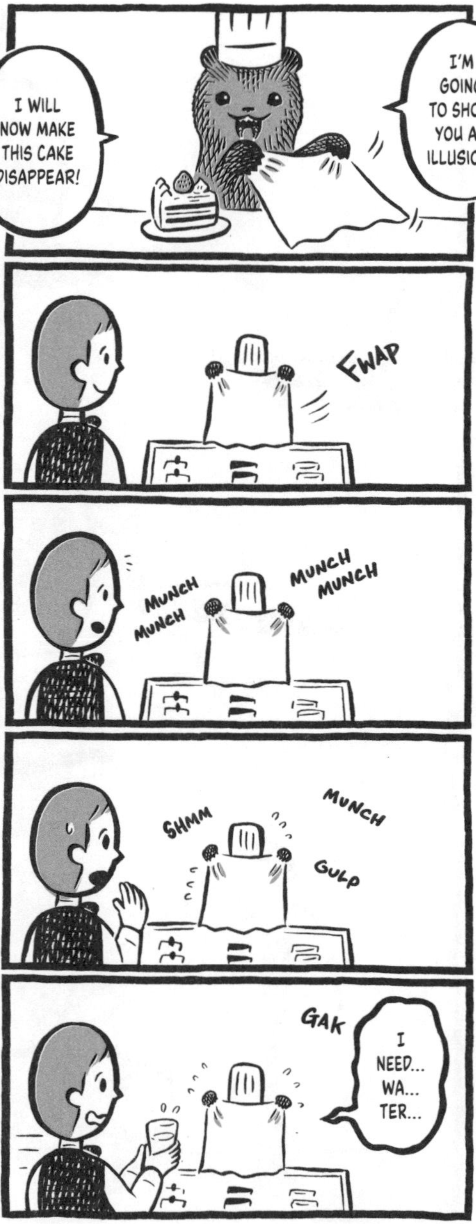
I'M GOING TO SHOW YOU AN ILLUSION!
I WILL NOW MAKE THIS CAKE DISAPPEAR!
FWAP
MUNCH MUNCH
MUNCH MUNCH
MUNCH
SHMM
GULP
GAK
I NEED... WA... TER...

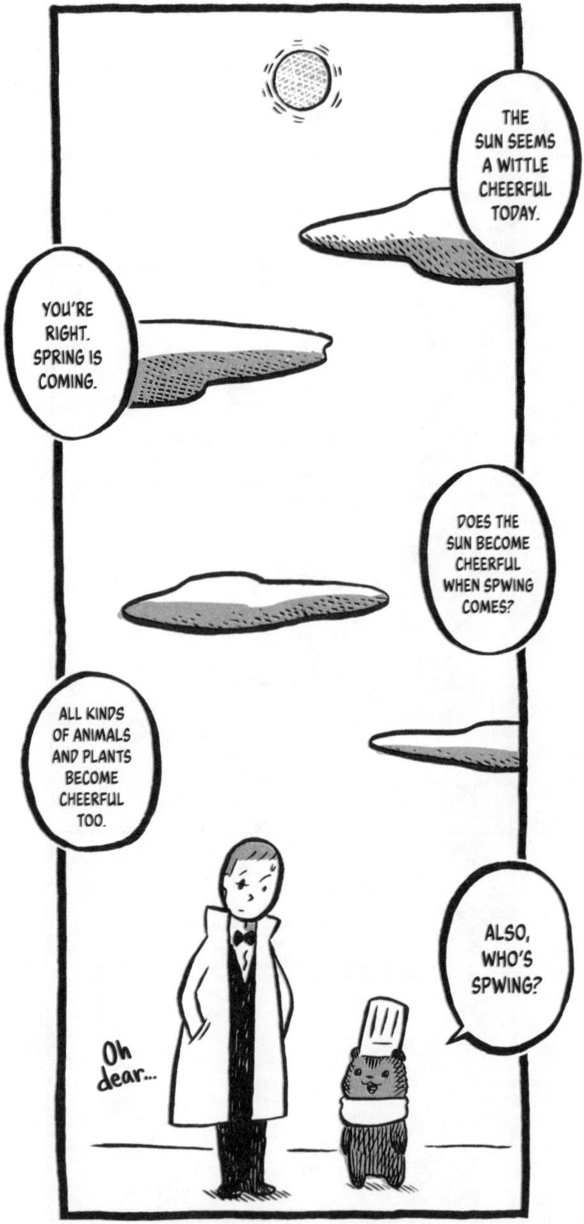
THE SUN SEEMS A WITTLE CHEERFUL TODAY.
YOU'RE RIGHT. SPRING IS COMING.
DOES THE SUN BECOME CHEERFUL WHEN SPWING COMES?
ALL KINDS OF ANIMALS AND PLANTS BECOME CHEERFUL TOO.
ALSO, WHO'S SPWING?
Oh dear...

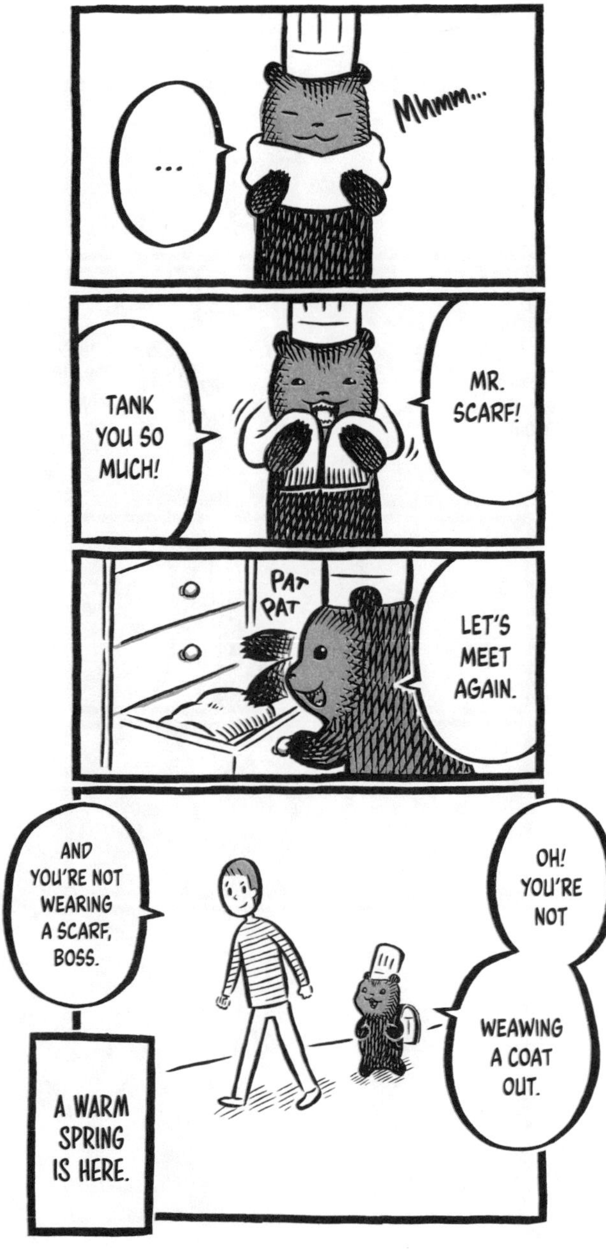
Mhmm...
...
MR. SCARF!
TANK YOU SO MUCH!
LET'S MEET AGAIN.
PAT PAT
OH! YOU'RE NOT
WEAWING A COAT OUT.
AND YOU'RE NOT WEARING A SCARF, BOSS.
A WARM SPRING IS HERE.

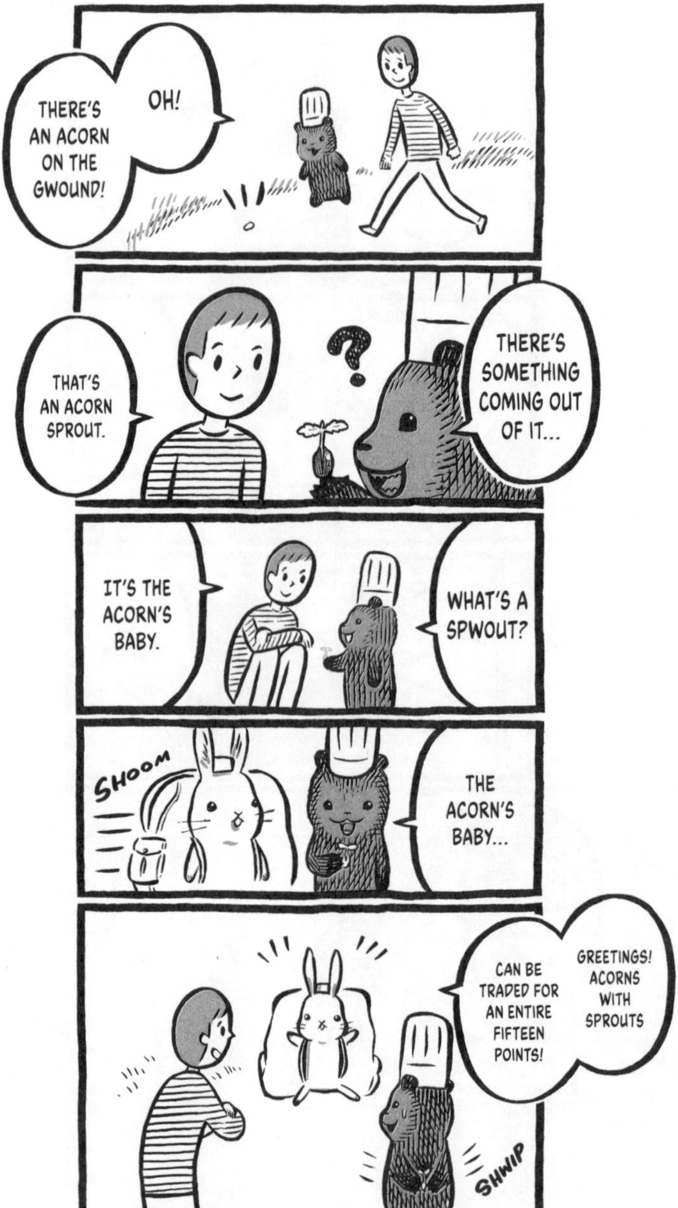
OH!
THERE'S AN ACORN ON THE GWOUND!
THERE'S SOMETHING COMING OUT OF IT...
THAT'S AN ACORN SPROUT.
WHAT'S A SPWOUT?
IT'S THE ACORN'S BABY.
THE ACORN'S BABY...
SHOOM
GREETINGS! ACORNS WITH SPROUTS
CAN BE TRADED FOR AN ENTIRE FIFTEEN POINTS!
SHWIP

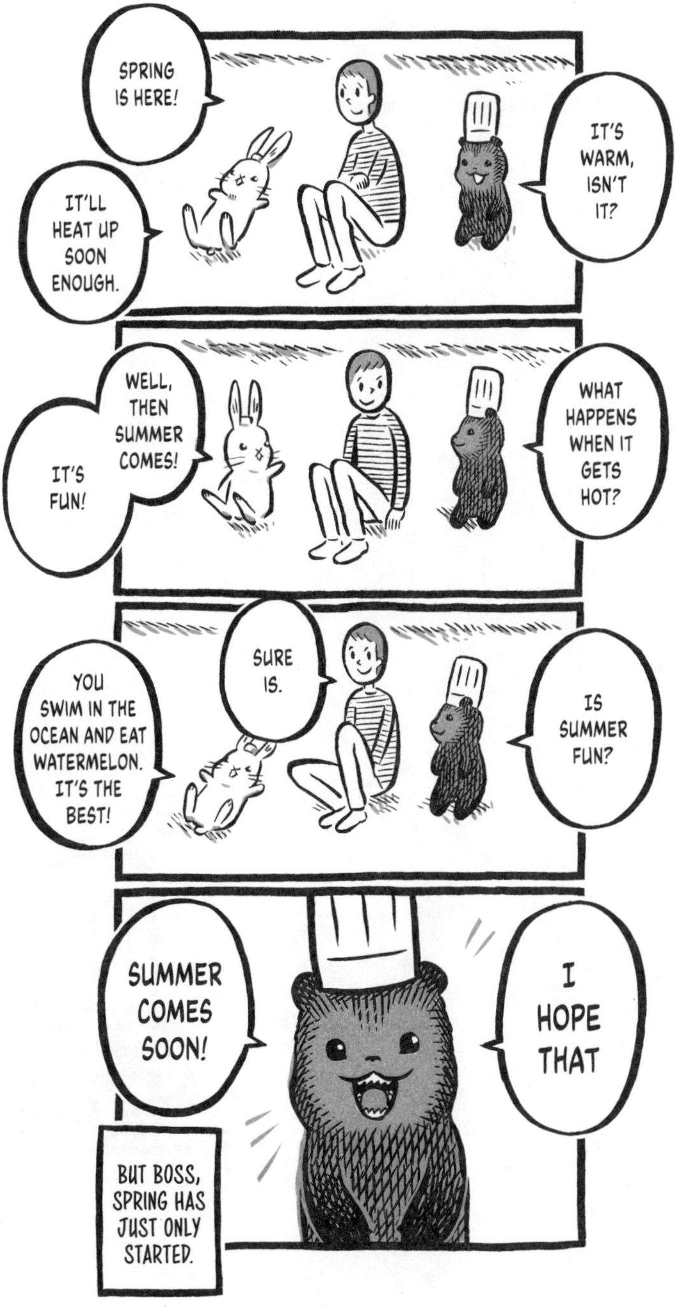
IT'S WARM, ISN'T IT?
SPRING IS HERE!
IT'LL HEAT UP SOON ENOUGH.
WHAT HAPPENS WHEN IT GETS HOT?
WELL, THEN SUMMER COMES!
IT'S FUN!
IS SUMMER FUN?
SURE IS.
YOU SWIM IN THE OCEAN AND EAT WATERMELON. IT'S THE BEST!
I HOPE THAT
SUMMER COMES SOON!
BUT BOSS, SPRING HAS JUST ONLY STARTED.

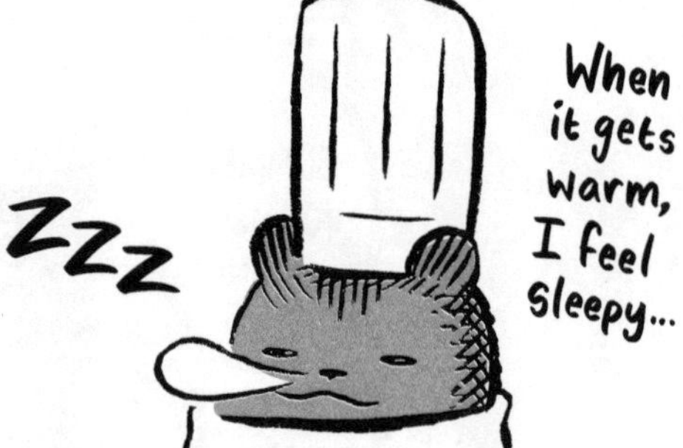
ZZZ
When it gets warm, I feel sleepy...

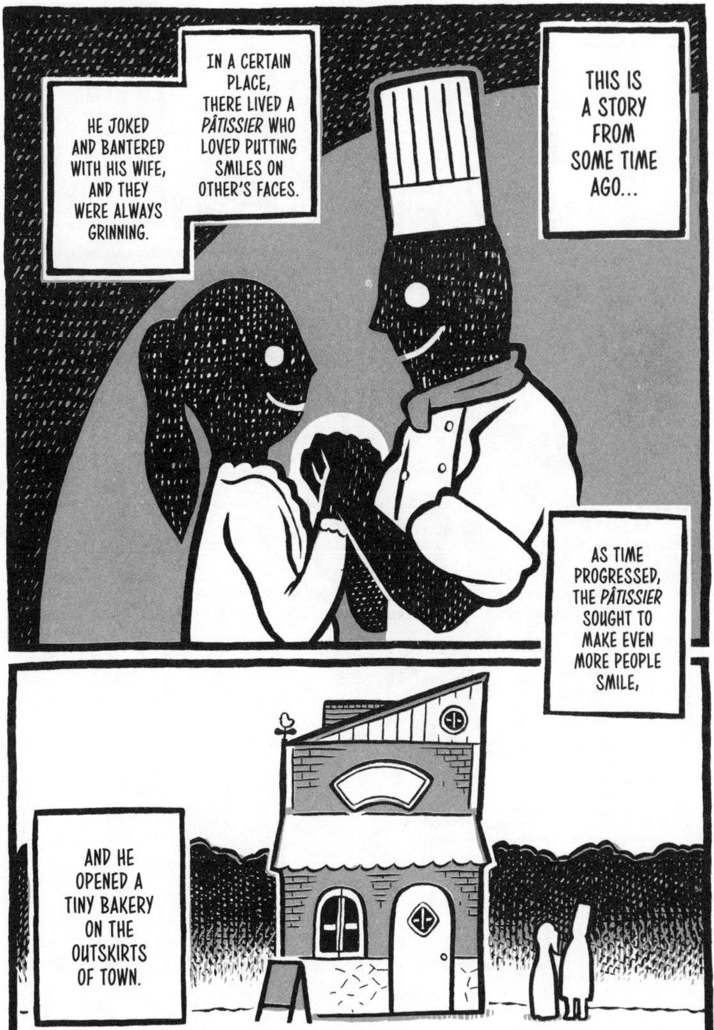
THIS IS A STORY FROM SOME TIME AGO...
IN A CERTAIN PLACE, THERE LIVED A *PÂTISSIER* WHO LOVED PUTTING SMILES ON OTHER'S FACES.
HE JOKED AND BANTERED WITH HIS WIFE, AND THEY WERE ALWAYS GRINNING.
AS TIME PROGRESSED, THE *PÂTISSIER* SOUGHT TO MAKE EVEN MORE PEOPLE SMILE,
AND HE OPENED A TINY BAKERY ON THE OUTSKIRTS OF TOWN.

CAKE BAKING WAS SUCH ARDUOUS WORK
BUT IT PUT SMILES ON SO MANY PEOPLE'S FACES, HE DIDN'T MIND.
THE CAKES THE *PÂTISSIER* MADE WERE SO SWEET AND DELICIOUS,
THAT THEY PUT SMILES ON COUNTLESS CUSTOMER'S FACES.
THE *PÂTISSIER*, WHO WANTED TO PUT SMILES ON MORE AND MORE FACES,
OPENED A MUCH LARGER BAKERY IN ANOTHER LOCATION.

HE WANTED TO MAKE IT BIGGER. HE WANTED MORE SMILES.

THE *PÂTISSIER* WORKED DILIGENTLY AND INDUST-RIOUSLY EVERY DAY.

THEN, AT SOME POINT, THE *PÂTISSIER'S* BAKERY HAD BECOME THE LARGEST IN THE WORLD.

ONE DAY,
A LETTER
ARRIVED
FOR HIM.

A LETTER
INFORMING
HIM THAT
HIS WIFE
HAD PASSED
AWAY.

WHAT WOE!
THE *PÂTISSIER*
WHO LOVED
MAKING
OTHERS
SMILE

HAD
NEGLECTED
TO MAKE
HIS MOST
BELOVED
PERSON
SMILE.

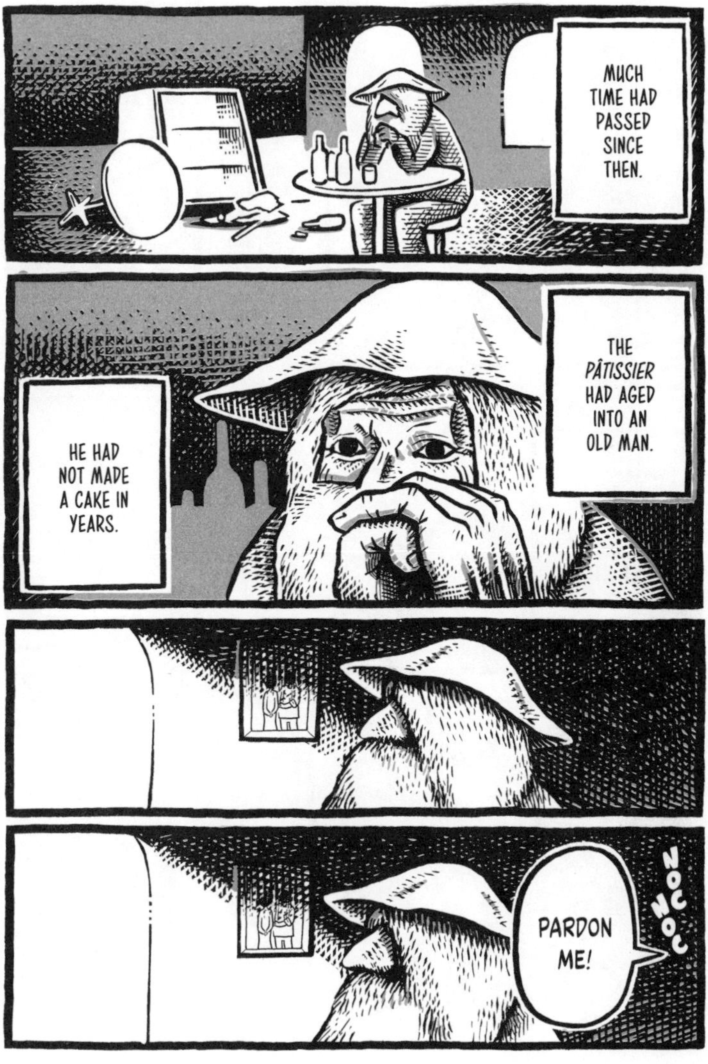
MUCH TIME HAD PASSED SINCE THEN.
THE *PÂTISSIER* HAD AGED INTO AN OLD MAN.
HE HAD NOT MADE A CAKE IN YEARS.
NOC NOC
PARDON ME!

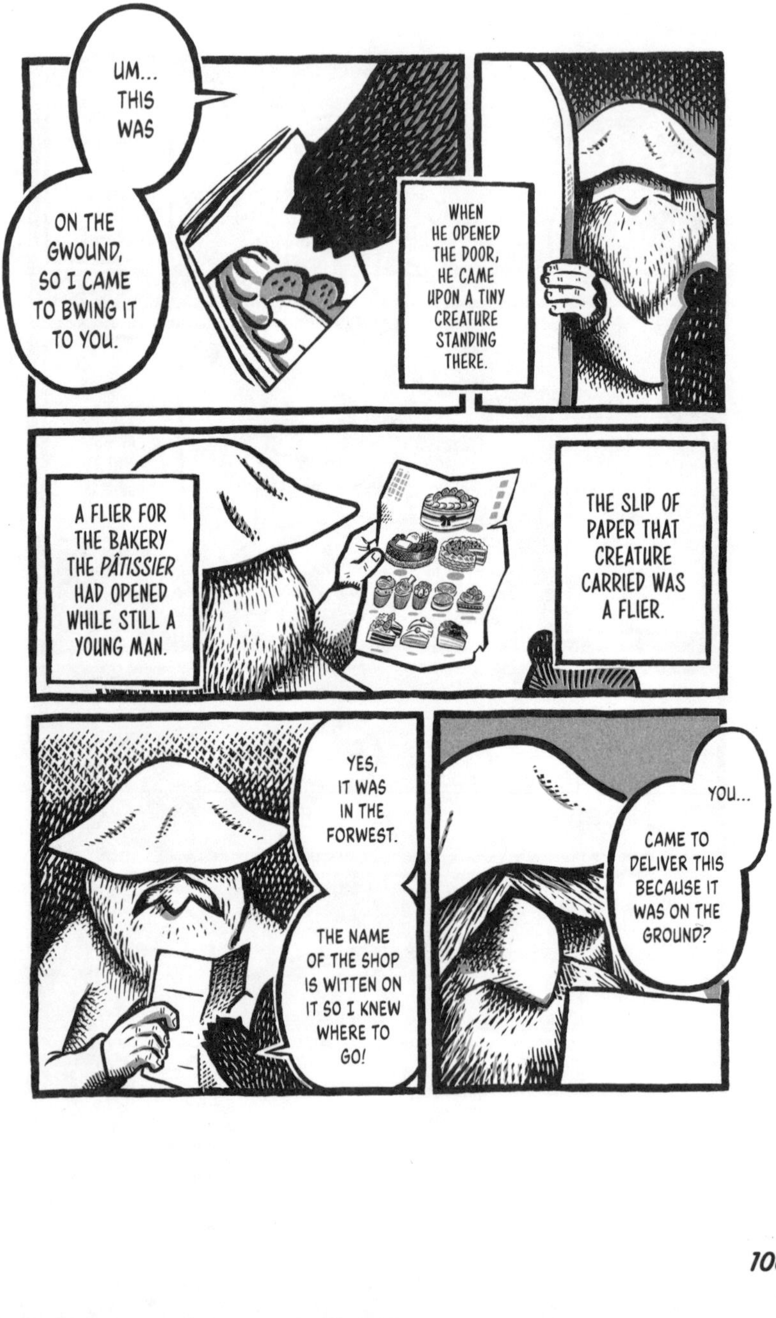
WHEN HE OPENED THE DOOR, HE CAME UPON A TINY CREATURE STANDING THERE.
UM... THIS WAS
ON THE GWOUND, SO I CAME TO BWING IT TO YOU.
THE SLIP OF PAPER THAT CREATURE CARRIED WAS A FLIER.
A FLIER FOR THE BAKERY THE *PÂTISSIER* HAD OPENED WHILE STILL A YOUNG MAN.
YOU...
CAME TO DELIVER THIS BECAUSE IT WAS ON THE GROUND?
YES, IT WAS IN THE FORWEST.
THE NAME OF THE SHOP IS WITTEN ON IT SO I KNEW WHERE TO GO!

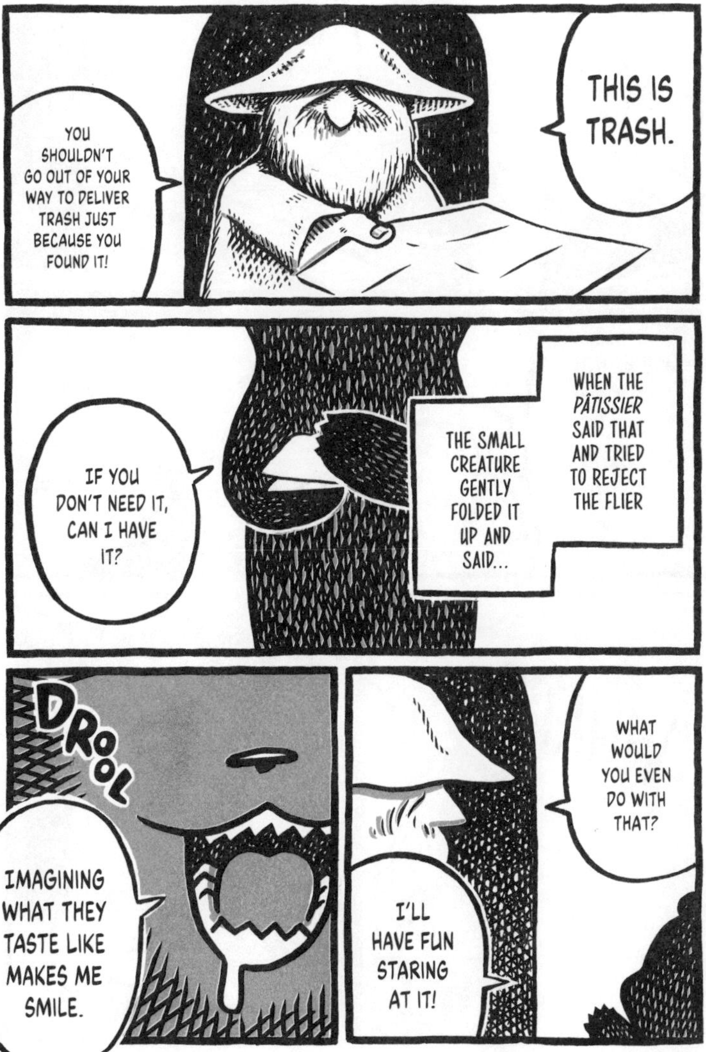
THIS IS TRASH.
YOU SHOULDN'T GO OUT OF YOUR WAY TO DELIVER TRASH JUST BECAUSE YOU FOUND IT!
WHEN THE *PÂTISSIER* SAID THAT AND TRIED TO REJECT THE FLIER
THE SMALL CREATURE GENTLY FOLDED IT UP AND SAID...
IF YOU DON'T NEED IT, CAN I HAVE IT?
WHAT WOULD YOU EVEN DO WITH THAT?
I'LL HAVE FUN STARING AT IT!
DROOL
IMAGINING WHAT THEY TASTE LIKE MAKES ME SMILE.

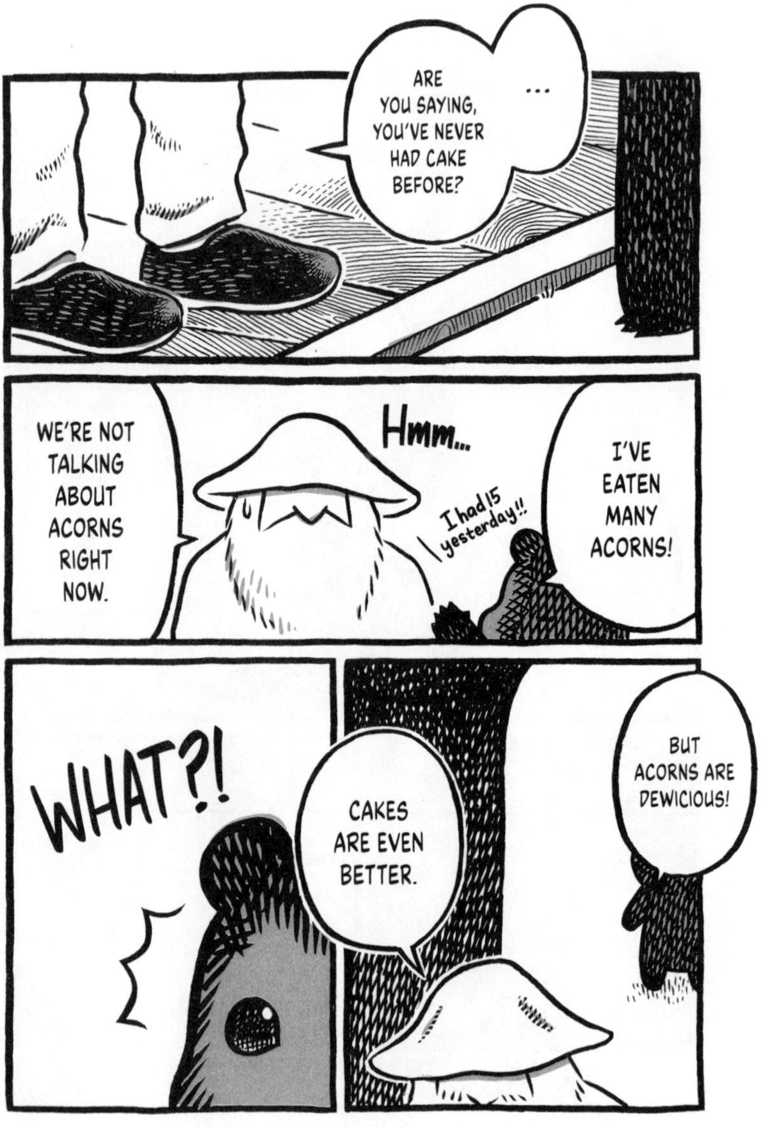
...
ARE YOU SAYING, YOU'VE NEVER HAD CAKE BEFORE?
I'VE EATEN MANY ACORNS!
I had 15 yesterday!!
Hmm...
WE'RE NOT TALKING ABOUT ACORNS RIGHT NOW.
BUT ACORNS ARE DEWICIOUS!
CAKES ARE EVEN BETTER.
WHAT?!

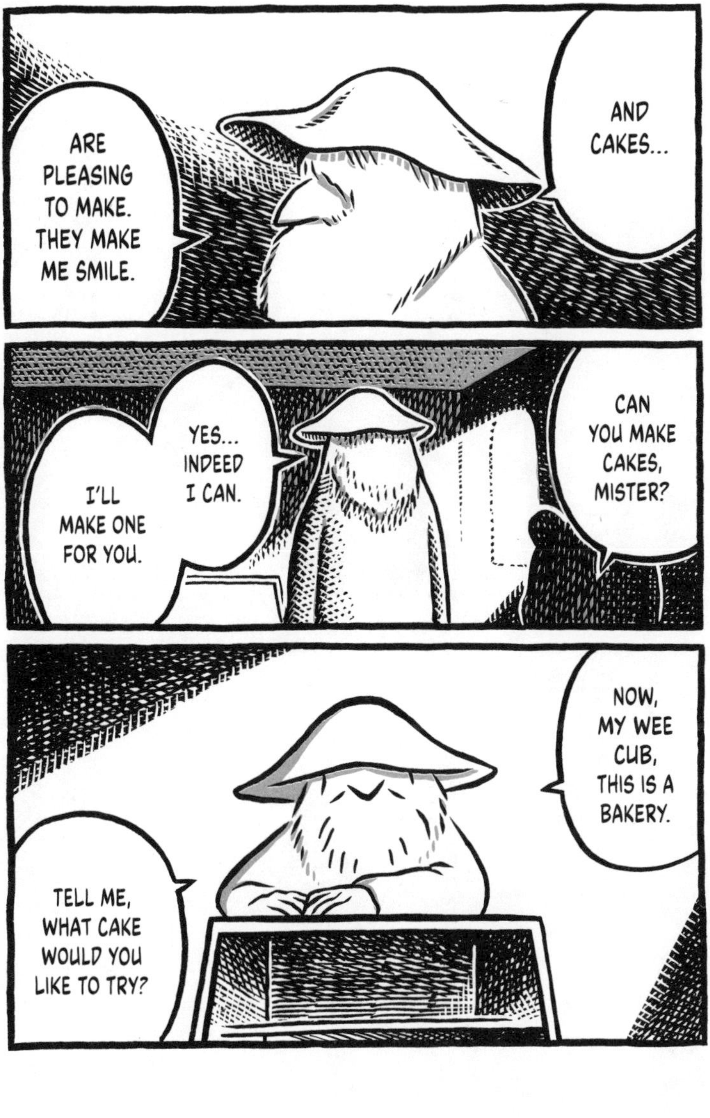
AND CAKES...
ARE PLEASING TO MAKE. THEY MAKE ME SMILE.
CAN YOU MAKE CAKES, MISTER?
YES... INDEED I CAN.
I'LL MAKE ONE FOR YOU.
NOW, MY WEE CUB, THIS IS A BAKERY.
TELL ME, WHAT CAKE WOULD YOU LIKE TO TRY?

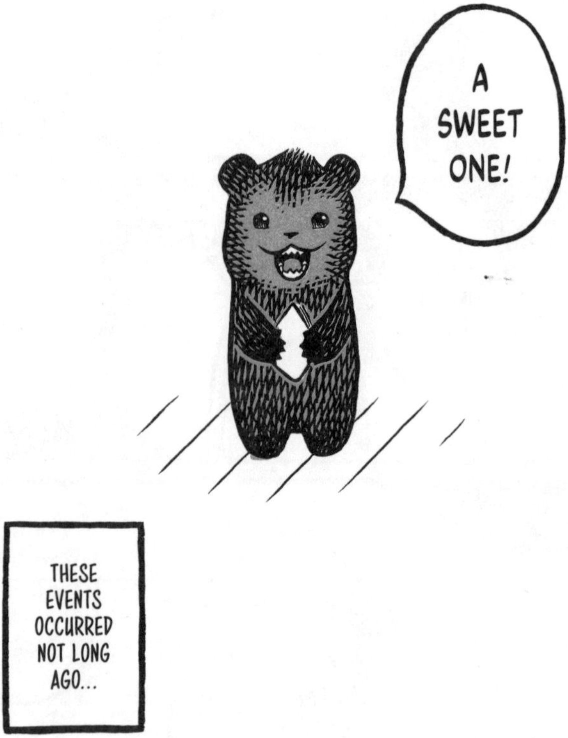
A SWEET ONE!
THESE EVENTS OCCURRED NOT LONG AGO...

BABY BEAR'S BAKERY

Part 1

Translator:	Jan Mitsuko Cash
Proofreading:	Patrick Sutton
Production:	Nicole Dochych
	Mo Harrison
Original Cover Design:	Naoko NAKUI

KOGUMA NO CAKE-YA-SAN Vol.1
by KAMENTOTSU
©2018 KAMENTOTSU
All rights reserved.
Original Japanese edition published by SHOGAKUKAN.
English translation rights in the United States of America, Canada,
the United Kingdom, Ireland, Australia and New Zealand arranged with
SHOGAKUKAN through Tuttle-Mori Agency, Inc.
Published in English by DENPA, LLC., Portland, Oregon 2021

Originally published in Japanese as *Koguma no Cake-ya-san*
by SHOGAKUKAN 2018

This is a work of fiction.

ISBN-13: 978-1-63442-980-1
Library of Congress Control Number: 2021943386
Printed in the USA

First Edition

Denpa, LLC.
625 NW 17th Ave
Portland, OR 97209
www.denpa.pub